Karla S. Rugh, D.V.M., Ph.D.

Miniature
Schnauzers

Everything About Purchase,
Care, Nutrition, and Behavior

D1311540

BARRON'S

2 CONTENTS

MEET THE MINIATURE SCHNAUZER

Introducing the Miniature Schnauzer: a lively, intelligent dog with working-class roots and a penchant for having fun.

The Schnauzer Family History

The Miniature Schnauzer shares a common heritage with its larger relatives, the Standard Schnauzer and the Giant Schnauzer. Schnauzers originated in Germany more than 600 years ago. A 14th-century statue at Mechlinburg, Germany, depicts a hunter with a Schnauzer crouching at his feet. Schnauzers also appear in art of the 15th and 16th centuries.

Schnauzers were developed by crossing the black German Poodle and gray Wolf Spitz with wirehaired Pinscher dogs. From the Pinscher the Schnauzer inherited the tendency for a fawn-colored undercoat, while the wiry salt-and-pepper coat so common in modern Schnauzers has been attributed to the influence of the Wolf Spitz. One of the contributions of the Poodle is the black coat coloration,

and even today, Schnauzers of this coloration sometimes possess the soft coat of the Poodle.

In the United States, the Schnauzer was originally classified as a terrier. In Germany, however, they have always been considered working dogs. They were frequently used to pull the farm produce carts and guard them while in town. These sturdy farm dogs were also used to work livestock, including cattle, sheep, and hogs. The Schnauzer's other farm chores included catching rats ("ratting"), and Miniature Schnauzers in particular excelled at this activity. In Germany, the Schnauzer is highly regarded for its intelligence and courage. Many of them were used as dispatch carriers and Red Cross aides during World War II. They have also been used for police work in their native country.

The Miniature Schnauzer as a breed was not developed by simply crossing the smallest Standard Schnauzers to one another to

produce smaller dogs. Rather, Standard Schnauzers were crossed to Affenpinschers—small terrier-type dogs that are only about 10 inches (25 cm) tall at the shoulder.

Miniature Schnauzers were exhibited as a distinct breed in 1899. They have been bred in the United States since 1925, and the American Miniature Schnauzer Club was organized in 1933.

Miniature Schnauzers are members of the American Kennel Club (AKC) terrier group. The Standard Schnauzer and Giant Schnauzer are members of the AKC working dog group, a designation that reflects the true working heritage of this old and venerable canine family.

The Miniature Schnauzer Breed Standard

The AKC's Official Standard for the Miniature Schnauzer describes the temperament and physical characteristics of the ideal Miniature Schnauzer. This is the standard by which Minis are judged in AKC-recognized dog shows. Obvi-

ously, not many dogs meet all the criteria of the ideal MS—even dog show winners have faults. If, after reading the standard, you determine that your pal falls a little short of ideal in some categories, don't worry. She may never be a show-ring winner, but as long as she's got a good temperament—and most Miniature Schnauzers do—and is healthy, she'll be a perfect pet!

The information here is just a synopsis of the Official Standard. You can take a look at the complete standard online on the AKC's Web site (*www.akc.org*) or in *The Complete Dog Book*, which is available at bookstores and libraries.

General Appearance and Size: The Miniature Schnauzer is a robust, active dog that resembles the closely related Standard Schnauzer. She's sturdily built and nearly square in proportion—meaning her length (from chest to tail) and height at the withers (shoulders) are nearly equal. The Miniature Schnauzer should not be toyish, rangy, or coarse.

Head: The Miniature Schnauzer's head should be rectangular, with a slight decrease in width from the ears to the eyes, and from the eyes to the tip of the nose. The muzzle is strong (somewhat large) in proportion to the skull, ending in a moderately blunt manner. The Miniature Schnauzer's thick whiskers accentuate the head's overall rectangular shape. The head should not be coarse or cheeky.

Teeth: The Miniature Schnauzer's teeth meet in a scissors bite, with the inner surfaces of the upper front teeth touching the outer surfaces of the lower front teeth when the mouth is closed. It's a fault if the teeth don't meet in this way—for example, having an undershot jaw, overshot jaw, or level bite.

Eyes: The eyes of the Miniature Schnauzer should be small, dark brown, oval, and deeply set, with a keen expression. The expression should be one of alertness and intelligence. The eyes should not be large, prominent, or light-colored.

Ears: Miniature Schnauzers are not required to have cropped ears. If the ears are cropped, however, they should be identical in shape and length, with pointed tips. Their length should be in balance with the size of the head. The ears, which should have minimal flare along the outer edges, are carried with the inner edges perpendicular to the top of the skull. If the ears are uncropped, they should be small and V-shaped, folding close to the skull.

Neck: The Miniature Schnauzer's neck should be strong and well arched, blending smoothly into the shoulders.

Body: The body should be short and deep, with the brisket extending at least to the elbows. The ribs are well-sprung and deep. The underbody is not tucked up and the topline is straight, declining slightly from the withers to the base of the tail. The length from the chest to the buttocks should nearly equal the height at the shoulder, giving the Miniature Schnauzer a square appearance when viewed from the side.

Forequarters: The Miniature Schnauzer should have flat, sloping shoulders that are well laid back, with the tips of the shoulder blades in a nearly vertical line above the elbows when viewed from the side. The elbows should be set close to the body, and the ribs should spread gradually to allow the elbows to move close to the body. The Miniature Schnauzer's sturdily built forelegs are straight and parallel when viewed from all sides.

Hindquarters: The hindquarters, which have strong, slanting thighs, are well bent at the stifles (knees), with pasterns that are perpendicular to the ground. The hindquarters should be angled sufficiently to permit the hocks to extend beyond the tail when the dog is in stance (posed, as for showing). The hindquarters should not be overbuilt (overly muscled) or higher than the shoulders. Faults include sickle hocks, cow hocks, open hocks, or bowed hindquarters.

Feet: The Miniature Schnauzer's feet are short and round (cat feet), with arched, compact toes. The pads of the feet are thick and black.

Gait: When viewed from the front at a trot, the Miniature Schnauzer's forelegs move straight forward and the elbows stay close to the body. From the back, the hindlegs are also straight and travel in the same line as the forelegs. At a full trot, the forelegs and the hindlegs may tilt inward slightly, but this is usually hard to see in a Miniature Schnauzer that moves correctly. From the side, the forelegs have a good reach (extend well to the front) and the hindquarters have a strong drive with good pickup (action) of the hocks.

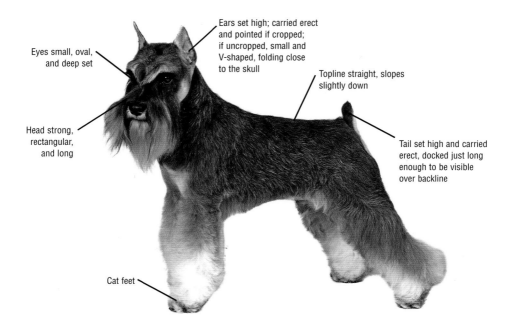

Ears set high; carried erect and pointed if cropped; if uncropped, small and V-shaped, folding close to the skull

Eyes small, oval, and deep set

Topline straight, slopes slightly down

Head strong, rectangular, and long

Tail set high and carried erect, docked just long enough to be visible over backline

Cat feet

Tail: The Miniature Schnauzer's tail is set high and carried erect. It is docked to a length that is just clearly visible over the topline when the dog is in proper length of coat.

Coat: The coat should be double with a hard, wiry outer layer and a close undercoat. The coat over the head, neck, and body must be plucked for shows. The furnishings—the long hair on the face and legs—are fairly thick but not silky.

Size: Miniature Schnauzers range from 12 to 14 inches in height. In dog shows, dogs outside these limits will be disqualified.

Color: There are three recognized colors of Miniature Schnauzers: salt and pepper, black and silver, and solid black.

The salt and pepper coloration is composed of a combination of black and white banded

hairs and solid black and white unbanded hairs, with the banded hair predominating. Some tan shading is acceptable. The salt and pepper mixture fades to light gray or silver-white in the eyebrows, whiskers, cheeks, under throat, inside ears, across chest, under tail, leg furnishings, inside legs, and underbody (optional). If the underbody is light-colored, the light coloration shouldn't come higher up on the sides of the body than the elbows. White markings of any kind are not allowed.

The black and silver coloration follows the same pattern as the salt and pepper, except the entire salt and pepper section must be black. No white markings are allowed.

Black is the only solid color allowed for a Miniature Schnauzer. The outer coat is a true black, while the undercoat is a less intense, soft matte black. The stripped portion of the coat should have no fading or discoloration, but the scissored and clipped areas may be a lighter shade of black. White markings are not allowed, except for a small white spot on the chest or occasional single white hairs elsewhere on the body.

Temperament: The Miniature Schnauzer is an alert, spirited dog that is obedient and willing to please. Friendliness and intelligence are characteristics of the breed. The Miniature Schnauzer should never be overly aggressive or shy.

To Crop or Not

Ear cropping is a surgical procedure in which the ear is trimmed to a pointed shape and made to stand upright. Originally, the ears of some dogs, usually fighting dogs and terriers, were cropped to keep them from being bitten by the dog's adversaries or prey. The practice gradually evolved into one performed solely for cosmetic purposes—to alter the appearance of the dog.

Ear cropping proponents argue that the procedure decreases the incidence of ear infections because the upright ear allows more air to reach the ear canal. Although ear infections can occur more frequently in some dogs with floppy ears, ear cropping is not performed to provide health benefits. Rather, it's done to alter the dog's appearance to conform to a preconceived image.

Some veterinarians refuse to perform ear cropping on the grounds that it is strictly a cosmetic procedure. In 2008, The American Veterinary Medical Association issued the following position statement: "The AVMA opposes ear cropping and tail docking of dogs when done solely for cosmetic purposes. The AVMA encourages the elimi-nation of ear cropping and tail docking from breed standards." The Canadian Veterinary Medical Association and the American Animal Hospital Association also oppose cosmetic ear cropping. The procedure is banned in the United Kingdom, Australia, and most European countries. The AKC supports the dog owner's right to make the decision about ear cropping.

The Miniature Schnauzer breed standard doesn't require cropped ears. If the owner elects to crop the puppy's ears, the procedure is usually performed at about 16 weeks of age. Under general anesthesia, the ears are trimmed and shaped, after which they are sutured. The procedure is quite painful. During the healing period, the ears must be carefully tended to prevent infection and promote proper healing.

Ear cropping should be performed only by qualified veterinarians, not by breeders or kennel personnel. If you decide to have your Miniature Schnauzer's ears cropped, take the time to find a veterinarian who is experienced with ear cropping. Poorly done ear crops are difficult, if not impossible, to correct. If a cropped ear becomes infected, it could become permanently misshapen.

As with so many other aspects of dog ownership, it is up to you to decide whether to have your Mini's ears cropped. Before you make your decision, review the pros and cons of the procedure. Examine the photos in this chapter, which illustrate the three types of MS ears: uncropped ears that stand up, uncropped ears that fold over, and cropped ears. You may find that you like the natural look better. Consider your puppy's personality and the effect of having a painful surgical procedure performed at such a young age. Finally, consider your ability and willingness to undertake any postoperative care that may be needed.

UNDERSTANDING YOUR MINIATURE SCHNAUZER

Miniature Schnauzers (and all domestic dogs) share more instincts with their wolf cousins than you might realize. Understanding some of these instincts will help you understand your Mini.

The Wolf Pack

Wolves are social animals, living and interacting with other wolves in an extended family group called a pack. The wolf pack inhabits a specific territory, the boundaries of which are marked by urination by the male wolves. The territory is fiercely guarded against other wolves. The pack hunts together, which is more effective than single hunting, and participates cooperatively in raising the young wolves.

The social order of the wolf pack is characterized by a hierarchy with one dominant (or alpha) male and subordinate males, which may themselves be dominant over more subordinate males. There is a similar social structure for the female wolves. The hierarchy of wolves is not constant; changes in dominance and subordinancy occur relatively frequently.

Each wolf's behavior is dictated by its social rank in the pack. The alpha male eats first, chooses his mate first (usually the alpha female), and all the subordinate wolves treat him with respect (at least until someone challenges his authority). This pecking order continues all the way down to the most subordinate wolf in the pack.

Canine Body Language

Dogs and their relatives communicate through complex and sometimes subtle movements that are readily understood by other dogs. Learning to interpret some of the most common canine body language will help you to better understand your Miniature Schnauzer.

It's not hard to recognize a happy dog. A happy dog approaches another individual (dog

or human) in a slightly crouching posture to acknowledge dominance of the individual it is approaching. The ears are back and the gaze is soft and indirect (an expression of subordinancy). The tail is usually wagging, but carried low. If the dog is approaching an individual that is much more dominant, it will often roll over on its back to expose its abdomen. This is the most submissive posture that a dog can adopt, and few others, even the most aggressive, will attack a dog in this position.

In contrast, an aggressive, dominant dog approaches another individual in a tense, upright posture, with head up and staring directly at the one being approached. The tail as well is held erect with little wagging. The lips may be drawn back in a partial snarl. If the dominant dog approaches another dog, the two may stand at right angles to one another in a type of canine showdown. If one dog does not immediately back down and demonstrate appropriate subordinate behavior, a dog fight may erupt.

Nervous behavior may be easy to identify but difficult to predict. Nervous dogs tend to vacillate between submissive and aggressive mannerisms, depending on the situation. Usually, however, a nervous dog will act submissive unless it perceives that its submissive signals are not being respected. Even then, the first course of action is usually to run away. If this fails, the nervous dog may threaten to snap or bite, but never with the body language of a truly dominant aggressive dog. Nervous dogs that become aggressive under circumstances such as these are often referred to as "fear biters."

Your Mini may not exhibit any of these behaviors as described, but if you watch closely you'll probably see examples of body language every day. Because dogs behave differently with different individuals, your pal may act happy and submissive toward you, yet become more dominant and aggressive around other dogs (or even other animals).

Today's Pack

For a domesticated dog, the human family becomes the pack. As in the canine pack, there is one dominant member and one or more subordinate members. The territory is, of course, the home and surrounding property, although some dogs may decide that the pack territory also includes highly frequented areas, such as the neighborhood park.

It's important for your Miniature Schnauzer to understand that his position in the family pack is one of subordinance to *all* humans, regardless of age or gender. To a dog, this is reassuring, not harsh. Remember: in a pack all of the members know their place. If your buddy understands the social order, he'll know how to act. A social order that constantly changes—for example, you allow dominant behavior on one day, but expect subordinance on the next—will confuse him.

It's easy to establish dominance with some dogs—these willing followers just tend to accept their position. Other dogs challenge authority every chance they get (hopefully your Mini isn't one of these).

So what can you do to prove that you're really the "top dog" in the family pack?

✔ Don't be too affectionate. Don't go overboard on the petting and coddling. In the canine world, the dominant member is aloof and displays little affection for subordinates. Instead, the subordinate members approach the dominant member and display affection.

So don't just pick up your Mini and start petting him. Call him to you and pet him only after he has obeyed a simple command, such as *sit*.

✔ Don't automatically respond to your pal's every wish. As the dominant pack member, you decide when it's time to eat or go outside (and you go through the door first).

✔ Don't feed your Mini before you eat. Subordinate pack members eat after the dominant ones.

✔ Don't let your buddy put his paws or head in your lap when you sit down. This is a dominant behavior similar to that displayed when a dominant dog puts its front paws on the subordinate dog's back.

✔ Don't allow him to be physically higher than you, such as on the back of your chair or curled around your neck. These are both dominant

behaviors and if you allow them, you'll confuse your friend about his place in the family pack.

By now you're probably thinking that all of this dominant-subordinate stuff sounds pretty serious and not at all fun. But remember, your Mini is very perceptive. Dogs are very good at interpreting social signals. You probably won't have to use all of these tactics to establish and maintain your dominance. Just acting like you're in charge will go a long way toward convincing your Mini that you're the boss. If, however, you find that you're losing a bit of your authority, it's nice to know how to regain it.

Your Mini and Other Family Members

Your Miniature Schnauzer's relationship with each family member depends on whether he perceives that person as dominant or subordi-

nate. Some dogs readily accept the husband as the dominant male, but view the wife and children as subordinate. In this case, the husband has little difficulty with the dog, but the wife and children encounter varying degrees of resistance to their requests. In a variation of this behavior, the dog acknowledges both the husband and wife as dominant, but regards the children as subordinate. Neither of these situations is acceptable: the dog is subordinate to every human family member, even children. To remedy this type of behavior, the dominant family member should pay extra attention to the "subordinate" members. In a wolf pack, association of a dominant wolf with a subordinate one elevates the status of the subordinate wolf. Conversely, the dominant family member should ignore the dog as much as possible to reinforce the dog's subordinate social position. Of course, you don't take these actions all the time—just when they're needed.

Some dogs act somewhat confused by children and exhibit neither consistently dominant nor subordinate behavior. This frequently occurs when the dog cannot interpret the child's actions or when the child doesn't understand (or simply ignores) the behavioral language of the dog. In addition, the boisterous activity of children, while joyfully joined by some dogs, may intimidate one that's shy or nervous. Even a normally quiet, friendly dog should be constantly supervised while around young children—for the protection of the dog as well as the child. Dogs that are prone to displays of dominant behavior often cannot ever be completely trusted around children of any age.

Sometimes a male dog treats the wife with particular deference while treating the husband as a subordinate. In extreme cases, the dog may even threaten the husband when he approaches his wife. Such behavior indicates that the dog perceives a pair relationship with the wife and views the husband as a rival. This entirely inappropriate behavior can be thwarted without violence by having the wife "reject" the dog by pointedly ignoring him. All dog care duties are turned over to the husband until the correct status quo is reestablished.

Your Mini and Other Pets

As you might guess, the meeting of two dogs is accompanied by all sorts of complex social signals. How your Miniature Schnauzer gets along with other dogs depends on a number of factors, such as the ages and genders of the dogs, where the meeting takes place, and whether either owner is present.

In general, dogs of different maturity stages (for example, puppies meeting adults) tend to establish an amicable relationship faster than dogs of similar maturity, unless both are puppies. Dogs of different genders seem to accept one another more readily, although this can vary widely depending on the specific situation. For instance, a female who is nursing a litter of puppies may be quite intolerant of a male dog.

A dog may be quicker to accept another if the meeting takes place on neutral ground, away from either dog's territory. Problems can arise, however, when either (or both) of the dogs decides that an oft-frequented public location, such as a park, is part of its territory. Finally, some dogs get along better when their owners are not around to precipitate problems arising from jealousy.

Your Miniature Schnauzer's behavior around pets other than dogs depends on both the pet and the particular situation. Despite stories to the contrary, many dogs get along quite well with cats, especially if they were raised together. In some cases, your Mini's response might depend on what the other pet is doing. For example, your pal might get along fine with a pet rabbit that's moving around quietly, but chase it if it runs. (Some dogs and other pets, especially cats, make a game of this, but be sure it is fun for both animals.) It's best, at least at first, to constantly supervise your Miniature Schnauzer and other pets when they are together, especially if there is a great size difference or one of the animals is capable of inflicting serious damage on the other. This latter situation is especially common when an adult cat takes offense at a puppy's advances.

Why Did My Mini Do That?

When I take my Miniature Schnauzer for a walk, why does he try to urinate on every tree we pass?"

Male dogs (and some female dogs) urinate to mark the boundaries of their territory. If another dog has previously urinated in a spot, your Mini will want to urinate there, too, to announce to other dogs that this is his turf. By the way, as the dominant member of your Mini's pack, you don't have to tolerate this behavior. Move him along with a reprimand and a quick tug on the leash.

Why did my Miniature Schnauzer try to bite me when I brushed his legs?

Although some owners attribute displays of this type to an unusual sensitivity to brushing, your Miniature Schnauzer may be trying to assert his dominance. You'll need to take steps to make

him understand that he's still subordinate to you. To do this, use some or all of the methods outlined earlier. In addition, teach him to obey a simple command, such as "sit" (see Training Your Miniature Schnauzer, page 79). After he's learned the command, have him sit while you gently brush him on part of his body where it least bothers him. When he tolerates the brushing, praise him. If he objects, stop brushing and give him the command to sit (this helps reestablish your dominance), then continue brushing. Gradually increase the duration and extent of brushing until he'll let you brush any part of his body.

I keep my Mini in a fenced yard but he still tries to chase my young neighbor when she goes by on her bicycle. Why?

This type of behavior mimics predatory chasing, only in this case the prey is the bicycling youngster, which your Mini may perceive as a single unit, rather than a human on a self-powered machine. Car chasing is a similar, and more dangerous, activity. Some dogs nip or snap at the object of their pursuit if they can get close enough. Others simply stop after a brief chase and bark in frustration. At any rate, it's always safest—for your Mini and the bicyclists—to keep your buddy on a leash or confined in a fenced yard.

Why did my Miniature Schnauzer growl at my three-year-old when she just walked into the kitchen where he was eating?

Your Mini's behavior indicates that he regards your daughter as subordinate—a totally inappropriate attitude in a human household, where the dog is subordinate to all humans, even children. Because of your daughter's age, you should intervene on her behalf, which will elevate her status in the eyes of your dog. You should also reinforce the family pack pecking order by using some of the previously described techniques for establishing dominance. Young children should never be left alone with a dog that exhibits any dominant tendencies toward them.

My Miniature Schnauzer gets along with the other dogs at obedience class, but won't tolerate my best friend's dog when we're at home. Why?

Dogs often behave differently away from their home territory. Your Miniature Schnauzer probably tolerates the other dogs at obedience class because he's in unfamiliar, neutral territory. At class, he's also in a situation that reinforces your dominant status over him, so he follows your lead—if you accept all the other dogs, then he'll do likewise. At home, it's a different story—this is his territory and he may have no intentions of welcoming a canine visitor.

"Why does my adult Mini always pick on our four-month-old puppy?"

Your older dog is asserting his dominance over the younger one. Although both dogs should be subordinate to the human family members, they will never be social equals—one will always be more dominant. Canine social status is not constant, so the dominant dog must continually reestablish dominance in response to the subordinate dog's attempts to gain it. As much as possible, you should allow your dogs to establish their own social order between themselves. Do not attempt to defend the subordinate dog (unless there is danger of real injury—a rare occurrence) because doing so will alter the social order between the dogs and ultimately cause more conflict.

SELECTING YOUR MINIATURE SCHNAUZER

You've finally made up your mind—you want a Miniature Schnauzer! Owning a dog is a huge responsibility; your Mini will need your care for its entire life. If you're ready for that kind of commitment, get set for a great adventure!

Pet Quality or Show Quality?

Before you go out in search of your ideal canine companion, you need to know what your ideal is. That way you're less likely to be swayed by a cute face or pretty color and to come home with a dog that really wasn't what you wanted.

What do you plan to do with your Miniature Schnauzer? First and foremost, you want a pet. If this isn't your first priority, then perhaps you should rethink your decision to get a dog. Dogs require human companionship; they shouldn't be bought and kept only as show or breeding animals.

It's perfectly okay to have a dog that's a pet as well as a show animal. If, however, you don't intend to show your Mini in conformation shows, there's no need to pay big bucks for a show-quality dog. Many Miniature Schnauzers aren't suitable for conformation showing. This doesn't mean that there's anything wrong with them; it simply means that they lack the physical characteristics required for success in the conformation show ring. Most of them make terrific pets, as long as they've got a good temperament. Besides, even if your pal doesn't quite match up to the AKC breed standard, you can still show her in competitions such as obedience trials or agility contests, where performance is the only thing that counts.

Breeders often sell pet-quality dogs with limited registration, which means that the dog is purebred but any puppies he or she produces cannot be registered. Breeders use limited registration to ensure that only those dogs that most closely meet the breed standard are allowed to reproduce. The AKC states that the litter owner (usually the breeder) is the only person who can

however, that even experts have a difficult time picking the puppy that will be a future winner.

Puppy or Adult?

Now you need to decide whether you want to adopt your Miniature Schnauzer as a puppy or an adult. There are advantages either way. What you decide depends on your expectations, your physical capabilities, your anticipated time commitment, and even your family's preference. For instance, a 23-year-old single woman may prefer a puppy, while a retired couple may feel more comfortable with an adult.

For many people, getting a dog means getting a puppy. It's easy to see why. Puppies are hard to resist—they're cute and cuddly. But puppies are also a lot of work. They eat several times a day. They chew things up, sometimes things that aren't so good for them. They must be house-trained. Like any youngster, puppies need supervision, both inside and outside. On the positive side, puppies quickly form strong attachments to their primary caregivers. This bonding can be the basis for a lifetime of love and companionship.

Adopting an adult Mini can be a unique and rewarding experience as well. It's easier to evaluate the personality traits of an adult dog. They're usually (not always!) calmer and more

limit registration or change a dog's status from limited to full registration. If your Mini has limited registration, you won't be able to show her in conformation shows, but you will be able to show her in any other AKC event.

You might decide you'd like to show your dog in conformation shows. If so, you'll need to purchase the best Mini you can possibly afford, remembering that you should *never* compromise temperament for physical perfection. A show-quality Miniature Schnauzer usually has parents that had successful show careers, although that's no guarantee of a show-quality puppy.

Unless you're a Miniature Schnauzer expert, you should rely on a knowledgeable breeder's opinion about the best puppy for showing. Keep in mind,

TIP

Just-Fine Print

The breeder may require you to have your pet-quality Mini spayed or neutered before giving you the registration papers.

"settled" than puppies. Adult dogs have already gone through the chewing stage. They're usually house-trained. If you want a show-quality Mini, you may want to purchase an adult because it will be easier to evaluate the physical characteristics. Some adults may also have show-ring experience. Miniature Schnauzers are friendly and outgoing by nature, but it may take a while for an adult to fully "adopt" its humans, particularly if the dog was strongly attached to its former owners. Nevertheless, once bonding occurs, the adult Mini will be as devoted to its new owner as it would have been had it been adopted as a puppy.

Male or Female?

You don't have to decide whether you want a male or female Mini before you go dog-shopping, but it helps to know the pros and cons of each. At least that way you'll know what to expect if your determination to select one gender gets blindsided by a particularly appealing individual of the opposite sex!

Male dogs in general are somewhat more aggressive than females, but this varies widely with the individual's temperament. As a breed, Miniature Schnauzers are not especially aggressive. Males tend to roam more than females and mark their territory by urinating on upright objects such as trees and telephone poles. Some males may raise their leg in the house, but this shouldn't be a problem if the dog has been reliably house-trained.

Female Minis, like females of other breeds, come into season ("heat," estrus) about twice a year. During this time, they can be bred, so confinement away from male dogs must be strictly enforced to avoid an unwanted litter. Females

in heat have a bloody vaginal discharge that may stain carpet and furniture.

Most gender-dependent disadvantages can be remedied by spaying or neutering. If you plan to show your Mini in conformation shows, however, spaying or neutering isn't an option since only intact dogs can compete in this type of show. Spayed and neutered dogs are eligible for other types of competition, such as obedience trials and agility trials.

Puppy Sources

Now that you've decided just what sort of Miniature Schnauzer you want, it's time to go shopping. For selection and quality, your best source for a new puppy or dog is a reputable Miniature Schnauzer breeder. These breeders strive to improve the Miniature Schnauzer breed by breeding the best dogs possible. Because their reputation depends on the dogs that they breed and sell, breeders go to great lengths to ensure that their puppies receive proper nutrition, socialization, and health care. In addition, the professional breeder maintains complete

records—registration papers, pedigree, show record, health record, and so on—for each dog.

Reputable breeders are very selective about the dogs they breed, so they usually have only a few puppies and adult dogs available (beware of the breeder that has dozens). Prices vary, depending on age and quality—for example, a pet-quality puppy will cost less than a show-quality adult. A reputable breeder tries to match the right dog or puppy to just the right owner. Breeders are also an invaluable source of information for new dog owners both at the time of purchase and afterward.

How do you find a Miniature Schnauzer breeder in your area? Check the following sources:

✔ Local dog clubs. Members of an all-breed club may be able to recommend a local Miniature Schnauzer breeder. In some areas, you may be lucky enough to find a dog club devoted solely to Minis.

✔ Veterinarians and groomers. These professionals often know local breeders.

✔ Pet supply stores. Talk to the store personnel and scout their bulletin board (if they have one) for breeder ads.

✔ Newspaper ads. This may or may not work, depending on your area. Some reputable breeders advertise in newspapers; others never do, preferring "word-of-mouth" advertising instead.

If you'd like to extend your search for the perfect Miniature Schnauzer beyond your local area, you can check major dog magazines, such as *Dog Fancy* or *Dog World*, or search the Internet. The Internet, in particular, offers a wide variety of breeder Web sites, which often contain detailed information about the breeding program, photographs of puppies and their parents, and even helpful hints about living with a Mini.

Questions to Ask the Breeder

- What health care have the puppies received? The puppies should have had their first immunizations and should have been dewormed. The breeder should also be able to tell you if the puppy you're considering has had any illnesses or injuries.
- Have you evaluated the temperament of each puppy? By knowing each puppy's personality, the breeder will be better able to help you pick out your new best friend.
- How have the puppies been socialized? Responsible breeders work diligently to make sure their puppies are well socialized and comfortable around people.
- Can I meet the sire (father) and dam (mother) of the puppies I'm considering? This can give you a good idea of how the puppy will look and act as an adult.
- Can I contact you in the future for information and advice about my MS? A responsible breeder doesn't mind answering questions at the time of purchase, or anytime after.
- If I can't keep my MS, will you take him back? Responsible breeders want their dogs to have good homes, even if they have to take one back. It's better to take the dog back than have it end up in an animal shelter or abandoned.
- Can you provide references? The breeder should be able to give you the names and phone numbers of previous buyers.

For many prospective dog owners, searching nationwide is impractical, because they may have to select the dog or puppy from photos or videos and have it shipped to its new home.

═══ **TIP** ═══

Long Distance

Don't hesitate to contact Miniature Schnauzer breeders outside your immediate area, even if you don't plan to make a long-distance purchase. A distant breeder may be able to put you in touch with someone in your area who raises Minis.

On the other hand, if you're reasonably certain that the breeder will have the perfect Mini for you, you might be willing to make a special trip to pick out your new friend and do the transporting yourself.

Rescue Organizations

Miniature Schnauzer rescue organizations help find good homes for Minis that have been rescued from shelters or abusive homes, or given up by owners who can no longer care for them. After the rescued Mini has been evaluated for health status and temperament, vaccinated, and spayed or neutered, volunteers try to find a new owner for it.

Adopting a Miniature Schnauzer from a rescue organization isn't for everyone. For one thing, most rescue dogs are adults, so if you want a puppy, you'll probably have to look elsewhere. Second, complete information about the dog's history and health status may not be available, although post-rescue evaluation and health care will minimize problems. Finally, some of the dogs need behavior modification or rehabilitation, depending on the rescue situation.

If, after considering these factors, you think you'd like to adopt a Mini from a rescue organization, contact the American Miniature Schnauzer Club to find a group near you. Some rescue organizations have Web sites with information about adoption procedures and, in some cases, pictures of available Minis. Rescue groups carefully screen prospective owners and counsel them about Miniature Schnauzer ownership. After adoption, they usually provide continued assistance throughout the Mini's lifetime. Many let owners return a dog they can no longer care for. The fees for adopting from a rescue organization are usually quite reasonable.

Choosing a Puppy

Once you've done all your homework, it's time for the fun—picking out your Mini. Choosing a puppy is special fun, but it can be very difficult to make up your mind; Mini puppies are so cute, you'll probably want them all! You can probably narrow the field a little if you know what to look for.

The ideal age to adopt a puppy is between 8 and 12 weeks. Puppies this age are usually weaned (if not, look elsewhere), eating well, and very energetic. They usually adapt quickly to their new home and form strong attachments to their new human family.

When you arrive at the breeder's home, take a minute to look around. Are the premises neat and clean? Do the puppies have a safe, fenced yard to play in? Do the puppies and other dogs look healthy and well-cared-for? If the answer to all these questions is yes, go ahead and look at the puppies. If, however, you find unkempt, dirty facilities and unhealthy dogs, do your puppy-shopping somewhere else.

When the breeder shows you the puppies, take a minute to observe them by themselves. Are they active and playful? Are there any that seem reluctant to join in? Are any of the puppies noticeably smaller than the others?

Finally, it's time to evaluate the puppies more directly. Get down on your knees and call them over to you, talking in a high-pitched voice and patting your knees. You should have a lapful of puppies almost immediately. Don't consider any puppy that doesn't come running to you. Look over the remaining puppies carefully. Do any of them seem more sociable than the others? Eliminate from consideration any puppy that seems timid or nervous.

Now pick each puppy up and examine it. The eyes should be clear and free from discharge.

There should be no evidence of nasal discharge. The gums should be pink, never pale. The puppy can have a bit of a tummy, but it shouldn't be pot-bellied, which can be a symptom of round-worms. Check to see if the puppy has an umbil-ical hernia, a small soft swelling near its "belly button." (Umbilical hernias, which aren't detri-mental to the health of the puppy unless they're quite large, can be repaired surgically. This isn't a problem in pet dogs that will be spayed or neutered, but some veterinarians won't perform this procedure on a dog that might be shown or bred, because it's an inherit-able condition.)

Male puppies should have both testicles in the scrotum by the time they're 12 weeks old. This may be difficult to assess, because there are muscles that pull the testicles up into the body when the puppy is stressed. A dog with an undescended testicle (cryptorchidism) cannot be shown in AKC conformation dog shows, and it's considered unethical for a veterinarian to rem-edy this condition by any means other than castration. Cryptorchidism isn't a major flaw in a pet-quality dog that will be neutered anyway, but abdominal surgery will be needed to remove the undescended testicle. (It should always be removed, because undescended testi-cles are more likely to develop cancer.)

Next, check the puppy's anal area. It should be clean and dry, with no signs of irritation, which could indicate diarrhea. Examine the puppy's tail—if it's been docked, it should be healed without oozing or excessive scarring.

As you examine each puppy individually, notice how it reacts to you. The puppy shouldn't be timid, but it should accept you as dominant. This means that it should allow you to perform your physical examination without protesting or nipping (wiggling is OK!). If the puppy protests vigorously or tries to bite, eliminate it from your search. While you hold the puppy, roll it over on its back in your lap and hold it there. It may struggle momentarily, but then it should lie quietly. Next, put the puppy on its feet on the floor or ground, place your hand over the back of its neck and shoulders, and gently push it down to a lying position. The puppy should accept this with minimal protest.

These maneuvers may seem odd, but they'll tell you a lot about the puppy's tractability—how well it will accept your authority. You defi-nitely don't want a puppy that is so timid that it plays dead every time you talk to it, but you also don't want one that challenges you all the time. The ideal is a friendly, outgoing puppy that readily accepts you as its leader. This type of puppy is usually lively, yet tractable and easy to train.

Once you've decided on your puppy, all that remains is to settle on a price (ideally, you've already discussed this with the breeder) and any conditions of the sale.

The breeder may want to remain in contact with you so he or she can keep up with how you and your new little friend are doing. If you plan to show your MS, the breeder will defi-nitely want to be updated on your progress.

Once all the official business has been con-ducted, it's time to gather up your brand new Miniature Schnauzer puppy and head for home. Don't be tempted to let your puppy have the run of the car. Use a carrier instead; it's a lot safer for both of you. Talk to your puppy on the way home. It will reassure your nervous traveler, plus it's a good way for the two of you to get better acquainted. After all, this is the begin-ning of a very special friendship!

LIVING WITH A MINIATURE SCHNAUZER

You're probably very excited—and a little bit scared—about your new Miniature Schnauzer. Don't worry— it won't take long to learn what your little friend needs. Then you can get down to the real fun: living with a Mini.

Essential Equipment

If you're like most dog lovers, you've probably always enjoyed looking at all the necessities and luxuries for dogs in the pet supply store. Finally, you have a reason to buy some of those items.

First of all, you'll need a food dish and a water bowl or bottle. Feeding paraphernalia needn't be fancy or expensive. A wide-based dog bowl made of crockery, plastic, or stainless steel can be used for food or water. Crockery bowls work well because they're heavy and can't be tipped over as easily as ones made of plastic or stainless steel. Instead of using a bowl for water, you can also use a water bottle set-up to eliminate spilling. Some stores carry suction-footed racks for food and water bowls.

You'll also need to buy a carrier or crate for your puppy's indoor bed. These products are often constructed of molded plastic or wire mesh. Wire mesh is convenient because you can raise it up on wood blocks or rails, which allows urine to drain out if your puppy has an "accident" in the carrier. Mesh isn't as comfortable as a solid floor, but your Mini probably won't mind as long as he has a soft blanket to curl up on. If you choose a molded plastic carrier, you may be able to purchase a mesh floor for it.

Now walk over to the collar and leash section of the store. Don't get a fancy collar right now, because your puppy will quickly outgrow it; a simple buckle-on nylon one will do for now. You can select either a nylon web or leather leash, since this is pretty much a one-size-fits-all item (don't make it too long—5 to 6 feet [1.5-1.8 m] is fine). Don't get a chain leash; it could hurt your buddy if it flips across his face or gets wrapped around a leg.

Puppy-Proofing Your Home

Once you're all set up to provide the basics of food and shelter, you'll need to puppy-proof your home (or at least the areas where your puppy will be). This is difficult, because Miniature Schnauzer puppies are small and can wiggle into very small spaces. Still, by combining vigilance and puppy-proofing, you should be able to keep your little investigator safe.

✔ Unplug all unnecessary electrical cords. Hide the necessary ones behind furniture, if possible. One good chomp and your little one will be on the receiving end of a nasty shock.

✔ Remove small objects such as paper clips, erasers, and marbles from your puppy's area. Puppies, like babies, put everything in their mouths and small objects of any kind are choking hazards.

✔ Don't leave string, yarn, thread, or cord where your puppy can get to it. These materials are extremely dangerous if chewed on and swallowed; they can cause severe damage to the digestive tract, which often requires surgery to correct. Long cords, such as those attached to draperies or blinds, could strangle your Mini youngster if he gets tangled up in them.

✔ Move your houseplants out of your puppy's area. Many houseplants, including dieffenbachia (dumb cane), philodendron, and pothos, are toxic to dogs. Other less toxic plants can upset your puppy's digestive tract if he munches down on the leaves or flowers. Rather than worry about which plants are toxic and which aren't, it's easier to simply remove them all until your puppy's urge to browse subsides.

✔ Keep all products such as paint thinner, antifreeze, cleaning products, and pesticides away from your puppy's area. All of these products can be fatal, sometimes in very small amounts. Don't

---

TIP

Crate Size

Choose a crate or carrier that's big enough for your Mini to easily stand up and turn around in, but not so big that he can eliminate in one end and sleep in the other. For a puppy, choose an adult-sized crate and put in a partition that can be moved (and eventually removed) as your pal grows.

---

be fooled by the fact that they smell awful and probably taste worse. You'd be amazed at the things a puppy will taste or chew up!

That Special Spot

Your newest family member needs a comfortable bed set up in a room or area that will be his special spot—a place to sleep and a cozy retreat away from the hustle and bustle of the household. Use a carrier or crate, lined with newspapers and soft towels or blankets, as a bed. That way, if you use the direct method of house-training, your puppy will already be accustomed to being confined in a carrier. Using a carrier as a bed also keeps the puppy in bed at night, which will help him learn that he has his own place to sleep—and it's not on your bed! Make sure the crate or carrier is equipped with a water holder so that your puppy always has free access to water.

Place the crate in a quiet area away from the major traffic areas of the house. Plan to leave the crate in that spot. You might want to place the crate in an area that isn't too close to the bedroom area of the house. That way, you'll know if your little one cries at night, but he won't be howling just outside your bedroom door.

Happy Homecoming

At last, it's time to bring your puppy home. When you do, remember that your mini is likely to be a little nervous. After all, it's all new to him. It'll take him a while to get used to his new home.

First, show your newcomer his bed, as well as his food and water dishes. (He'll be more impressed if there's a little snack and some water in the dishes.)

Then let him explore his surroundings. Let him choose his own pace—he may want to stay right next to you for awhile or he may immediately begin to check out the territory. Don't let other family members, who may be understandably excited by this new addition, interfere during his exploration. They can watch, of course, but it's better to let your newcomer go at his own pace. Let him decide when to approach the family members, not the other way around. For the time being, remove other dogs and cats from the puppy's area. You'll have plenty of time to introduce them later (Remember, your puppy might not even know what a cat is!). Don't get upset if your new buddy has an accident on the floor—that's normal for an excited puppy.

Once your puppy has explored the house and met the family, he may be ready for a nap. Then again, he may want to play a bit. That's okay; just don't overdo it. He's just a baby and he'll tire rapidly, especially today, when he's stressed from all the changes in his life. Be particularly careful about allowing young children to handle him and play with him. Puppies are so much

fun that it's hard for children (and some adults) to stop playing with them, even when the puppy is obviously exhausted.

Sweet Dreams

Your Mini puppy may have a little trouble sleeping the first night. Can you blame him? After all, this is his first night in a new home, away from his mom and his brothers and sisters. He's probably never slept by himself. Does this mean you should take him to bed with you or maybe bring his bed into your bedroom? Absolutely not. It may sound heartless, but the quickest way to get him used to sleeping where he belongs—in his own bed in his own special can lodge in the digestive tract and cause obstruction. For this reason, it's safest to give your Mini large rawhide chews, which aren't easily gulped, or thin strips, which can be bitten off in small pieces. Monitor your pal's chewing activity. If he bites off big chunks of his rawhide chew, replace it with a larger one or a chew made of a different material.

Pig's ears: Dried pig's ears, which are sometimes smoked, also appeal to many dogs. These products are similar to rawhide items. The smoking process may enhance the chew's appeal, at least for some dogs, but this may be more of a marketing gimmick than anything else.

Chew bones: You can also find a variety of natural and artificial chew bones at your pet supply store. Some of these are entire beef bones, which have been specially processed and smoked for added appeal. Nonedible artificial chew bones are made of nylon, rubber, or other materials that have been treated to appeal to dogs. These products are safe for your MS because they offer the satisfaction of bone chewing without any of the dangers. Edible artificial chew bones can be eaten without ill effects. Some pet supply stores also carry dried cattle hooves, which are very popular with dogs. In fact, horseshoers often work in the presence of the farm dogs, who regard hoof trimmings as an extra-special treat!

Balls: Balls are fun for dogs of all ages. Choose a ball that's made of hard rubber. It should be solid or have thick enough walls that it can't be torn open and chewed up. If it has a bell or squeaker, make sure it's safely sealed inside. The ball should be somewhat large for your Miniature Schnauzer's mouth. If the ball is too small, it could be swallowed and cause a digestive tract obstruction.

In addition, your Mini could choke if he got an undersized ball stuck in the back of his throat (for this reason, always bounce a ball to your pal, instead of throwing it directly to him).

Name, Rank, and Serial Number

Every day, dogs wander away from home and are never seen again by their owners simply because there was no way to identify them. Your Miniature Schnauzer should wear some form of identification at all times. Even if he's always in a fenced yard or on a leash, don't gamble that he won't escape. Adequate identification is especially important for Miniature Schnauzers because they have few distinguishing characteristics such as spots, white markings, or unusual coloration. Sure, you can easily identify your pal, but to a casual observer, he may be just another little gray Schnauzer.

Identification for your Mini doesn't have to be elaborate. It could be as simple as your phone number scratched on the metal plate of his collar. You could have a special identification tag made that gives your name, address, and phone number. Even a rabies vaccination tag can serve as identification if the veterinary clinic where the vaccination was administered (listed on the tag) records the tag number along with the owner's name. Tags are better than no identification at all, but they can be easily lost or removed because they are attached to the dog's collar. If the collar comes off, so does the identification. Because of this, a tag won't protect your Mini from being stolen.

Tattooing

Another method of identification is tattooing, which can be done by a veterinarian. Your phone number or other information can be tattooed on the inside of your Mini's ear or on his abdomen. Tattooing offers more security against theft than collars and tags, but it doesn't provide absolute protection because tattoos can fade and alteration is possible.

Microchipping: Microchipping—implantation of a data chip under the skin on the back of the neck—is the most sophisticated means of identification. The microchip, which is about the size of a grain of rice, contains an identification number that can be read with a special scanner. The identification number, along with owner identification, is registered in a database maintained by the microchip manufacturer or other lost dog program, such as the AKC Companion Animal Recovery Program. Someone who finds a lost dog can't tell if it's been microchipped (and wouldn't be able to access the information if they did know), but many animal shelters and veterinary clinics have microchip scanners. The average person can't remove or alter a microchip; because of this, microchipping offers the best security against dog theft.

The Great Outdoors

Most dogs enjoy being outdoors, but you can't just shove your Mini out the door. He needs a safe place to play and relax, an area with shade, shelter, comfy lounging spots, and free access to water (and food, if he's outside at mealtime). Grass is cooler and more comfortable on the paws, but a concrete surface has advantages too: it's easier to clean and less likely to harbor fleas, ticks, and internal parasites. If the play area has a hard surface, be sure to provide some soft bedding, in case your pal wants to take a nap.

The play area needs to be adequately fenced. Your Mini doesn't need a huge fence; 3½ to 4 feet (1–1.25 m) high should be sufficient, but it's better to err on the side of too high (it's hard to make a fence higher, unless you replace the whole thing). Chain link fences let the dog see beyond the yard. Some dogs, however, become adept at climbing chain link fences because they can get good toeholds in the mesh. This usually isn't a problem if the fence is high enough.

Invisible Fences

You could also install an invisible fence to keep your buddy in your yard. Invisible fences operate on radio waves. The dog wears a special collar that picks up a signal emitted from a wire that has been buried around the perimeter of the yard. When the dog approaches the perimeter, the fence emits a high-frequency warning sound. If the dog stops, nothing happens. If he continues toward the perimeter, the collar emits

a brief shock that's uncomfortable, but not painful. The dog quickly learns to turn away when he hears the warning signal. An invisible fence provides effective restraint only if all of the components work correctly and the dog wears the collar. If any part of the fence fails or your Mini slips out of the collar, there's nothing to keep him in the yard.

It's important to realize that an invisible fence won't keep other dogs out of your yard, so your Mini will be especially vulnerable to dogs that are aggressive, sick, or apt to cause other problems. Not only that—if your pal happens to cross the fence line in a moment of excitement (for example, chasing a squirrel), he won't want to return to the yard because he'll get shocked.

Puppy-proofing Your Yard

You will need to puppy-proof (or dog-proof) your Miniature Schnauzer's outside play area. Make sure there are no nails or other sharp objects protruding from boards or gates. Remove any ropes, cords, or strings from the area—these are strangling hazards and can be

dangerous if chewed and swallowed. Don't keep chemicals, pesticides, or plant fertilizers where your buddy can get to them.

Note: Puppies and dogs don't often chew or eat plants outside (there are just too many other things going on), but it's still a good idea to make sure the play area has no toxic plants, such as castor bean or oleander.

Walks

Of course, you're not always going to turn your Mini out in the backyard for exercise. Sometimes you'll want to go for walks together. Always keep your pal on a leash during your walks. It's far safer for your dog, even if he's well trained. You never know when he might spot a cat to chase—right into the path of an oncoming car. Or a canine bully may suddenly jump out from behind a bush and challenge your normally well-mannered buddy. Finally, you may be legally required to have your dog on a leash. Many towns have laws that prohibit free-ranging dogs off the owner's property.

Home Sweet Home

If your Miniature Schnauzer will spend more than a few minutes outside (for instance, during the day while you're at work), he'll need a doghouse. Doghouses are available at retail outlets, such as pet supply stores, hardware stores, and discount stores. If you're handy with tools, you can also build a doghouse for your buddy. If you have limited resources, check the classified ad section of your newspaper; sometimes you can find a quality doghouse at a bargain price.

Regardless of where you obtain it, the doghouse needs to be roomy enough that your Mini

can stand up and turn around in it, but not so large that he and several of his friends could throw a party inside. The house should be made of weather-impervious material to prevent leaks when it rains. It should also be insulated for winter warmth, if necessary. If the roof lifts off, your doghouse cleaning chores will be a lot easier.

Place the doghouse in a shady area that's as sheltered from the elements as possible. In most climates, the house should be positioned with the door facing south. This will shelter your Mini from cold north winds in the winter and allow the cooling southern breezes to enter the house in the summer. Place the house slightly off the ground on a platform or runners, but don't raise it too high—you don't want cold air circulating under the house in the winter.

Bed the house according to the weather. If it's summertime, a soft blanket or pad is sufficient. In the winter, bed the house more heavily with thicker blankets, cedar shaving-filled pads, or an electric heating mat designed for outdoor use (heating pads are safer than heat lamps).

Straw makes a soft, warm bed as long as you use enough. Fill the doghouse about one-third to one-half full of it (it will settle). Baled straw can be used to provide extra insulation for the doghouse, too. Simply stack the bales around the house.

Weather Extremes

Healthy adult dogs can tolerate cold weather far better than most people realize, *as long as they have been acclimated to it and have adequate shelter.* Your Miniature Schnauzer won't be comfortable at 40°F (4.4°C) if he has to sleep in the open, but if he's gradually gotten used to the cold, he'll easily tolerate zero degrees if he

has a dry doghouse that is properly insulated and bedded.

Of course, you may not want your pal to stay outside when it's very cold. Just try to be consistent—don't continually shift him back and forth from the warmth of your house to the cold outdoors (outdoor potty breaks and exercise sessions are okay). Veterinarians see more health problems in dogs handled like this than in dogs that spend the majority of their time in either one place or the other.

If your Mini spends a lot of time outside in cold weather, make sure he has adequate water. Provide fresh water several times a day or use a heat lamp or heated water bowl to keep the water from freezing. You'll also need to feed him more—those extra calories will help him stay warm.

In the summertime, you'll have just the opposite problem—how to keep your pal cool.

═══ **TIP** ═══

Car Smarts

Always confine your Mini in a carrier in the car. You'll both be safer. It's not acceptable to have someone else hold him: he could escape, with disastrous results.

Your Miniature Schnauzer will be able to tolerate hot weather as long as he has been acclimated to it and has ample water and shade.

Heatstroke

Dogs aren't particularly susceptible to heatstroke unless they're forced to remain in an environment where they can't dissipate excess body heat, such as in a car with closed windows. Unlike people, dogs seldom overexert themselves in hot weather, preferring instead

to lie around in the shade. Most dogs simply stop exercising when they get too hot.

If your Mini must stay outside in hot weather, be sure to provide plenty of water. Some dogs enjoy playing in shallow wading pools. A child's plastic wading pool with low sides works well for this. The water doesn't need to be deep—three or four inches is sufficient.

Riding in the Car

Some dogs, especially puppies, are prone to carsickness. Sooner or later, you'll need (or want) to take your Miniature Schnauzer somewhere in the car. Your pal may have an appointment with the veterinarian, or you may just want a change of scenery. Whatever the case, you'll need to get your Mini used to riding in the car before you go. Take your puppy for car rides frequently, starting out with short ones and gradually increasing the duration. Don't give up if your little friend is less than enthusiastic about car rides at first. If you do, his only car trips will be the necessary ones, such as visits to the veterinarian, and he really won't want to go. Instead, go fun places—the park, to a friend's house, to a farm.

Understandably, dogs that get car sick don't usually enjoy riding in the car. The signs of carsickness include restlessness, whining, profuse drooling, and vomiting. If your Mini is prone to carsickness, the following measures may help:

✔ Never feed your pal a big meal right before a car ride. A ginger snap or two might ward off car sickness, however, because ginger is a natural antiemetic.

✔ Start out with very short rides on smooth roads that don't have a lot of turns and hills.

✔ Reassure your puppy constantly during the ride. Carsickness can be worsened by anxiety.

✔ Maintain a happy demeanor, even if your pal gets sick. Your goal is to convince him that a car ride is fun, not something to dread.

As your little friend becomes more able to ride without carsickness, gradually increase the length of the trips, adding turns and hills to the routes. Most of the time, the tendency toward car sickness goes away as the puppy matures and becomes more experienced with riding in the car.

Boarding Your Miniature Schnauzer

Much as you and your Miniature Schnauzer enjoy spending time together, it may be inconvenient or impossible to take your buddy with you on a trip. When this happens, you'll need to find someone to take care of him while you're away. The options available to you depend on the length of your trip, your resources, and where you live.

You may be able to have a friend or neighbor take care of your Mini while you're gone. For short trips (two to three days), you might be able to leave your pal at home, with the caretaker coming in at least twice a day to feed, water, and exercise him. This works well for some dogs, but not so well for others. If your Mini isn't absolutely trustworthy at home alone, you'll need to isolate him in a dog-proofed area or you may return to find your house in shambles. For longer trips and dogs with questionable manners, it's better to have your Miniature Schnauzer stay at your friend's house.

In some towns, you can hire a professional dogsitter to come to your home and care for your Mini while you're gone. The pros and cons of using a dogsitter are similar to those for a friend performing in-home care, except a dogsitter will probably charge you more.

Boarding your Miniature Schnauzer at a kennel is another option. Before you do, however, you'll need to carefully investigate the boarding kennels in your area. There is often a wide disparity in their physical facilities, standard of care, and cleanliness. A reputable kennel will require that your dog be healthy and have up-to-date immunizations. The facility itself should be clean and well ventilated, with roomy cages and secure runs for individual exercise sessions. The personnel should be friendly, experienced, and obvious dog lovers. The boarded dogs should be content, healthy, and clean. Unfortunately, the concentration of a large number of dogs in a relatively small area increases the chances of spreading diseases such as kennel cough, even if the kennel has strict standards for health and cleanliness. Kennel cough—aggravating, but not usually serious—is probably the most common disease contracted at a kennel; the incidence of more serious ailments, such as distemper, is relatively rare at most reputable facilities.

You might be able to board your Mini at your veterinarian's hospital or clinic. The care and facilities at most veterinary clinics are usually very good—with the added advantage that veterinary care is readily available if your Mini needs it. This is a good option if your pal has a health condition, such as heart disease or epilepsy, that requires regular monitoring or medication. Like boarding kennels, veterinary clinics may have a relatively large number of dogs in a fairly small space. However, virtually all veterinary clinics isolate animals with contagious diseases away from those with noncommunicable problems. Some further isolate boarded animals away from the hospitalized ones.

The necessity of house-training is enough to make prospective dog owners think twice before adopting a puppy. It's understandable: a dog that's not reliably house-trained isn't much fun to have in the house. Add the inevitable house-training questions—how to do it, when to do it—and you have a situation that almost always creates tension for both the owner and the dog.

House-training your puppy isn't much different than teaching him to sit or heel. As with any training, it's going to take time for your youngster to learn what he needs to do.

House-training will go smoother if you make it easy for your puppy to choose the right behavior. It also helps if you take advantage of the basic canine instinct to keep the den clean.

House-training Tips

1. Don't just let your Mini out in the backyard. Take him outside to a place where he's relieved himself before (or where you want him to) and praise him when he does it again.

2. Puppies usually need to eliminate right after eating and right after they wake up, so take your Mini out at those times.

3. Don't punish your dog for accidents. A mild reprimand at

the time the accident occurs is enough. Don't scold him if you find a pile or puddle after the fact—he won't associate your correction with the act.

House-training will be easier if you wait until your Mini is at least four to six months old. At this age, he'll have the control and understanding needed for success. It's okay to start house-training earlier, but don't expect too much and don't get upset about accidents.

The direct method of house-training, which involves taking the puppy outside to relieve himself, is convenient for dog owners who have easy access to outdoors. It works best if the owner is often at home. Owners who live in apartments or who are frequently away from home may have more success using paper training as an intermediate step toward outside elimination.

Direct House-training

Before you start direct house-training, get your Mini a crate or carrier. Choose one that has enough space to turn around in, but not so big that your puppy can easily get away from any messes he makes. Line it with newspapers and towels or a blanket for a bed. Equip the carrier with a holder for a water bowl or bottle. It's important to make the crate as comfortable as possible so your puppy enjoys his time there.

With direct house-training, you'll take your puppy outside to relieve himself after eating, after naps, and any other time he shows signs of needing to go out. When you return to the house, confine your Mini to his crate. It's okay to keep him in a restricted space such as the kitchen, as long as you can watch him closely. If your puppy has an "accident," reprimand him mildly (if you catch him in the act), then take him outside to his potty spot. He'll soon learn that it's inappropriate (an unpleasant, if he's in his crate) to eliminate in the house.

Direct house-training is fast and efficient. Confinement may be difficult for both you and your Mini, but it only lasts a few weeks. It's far better than dragging out house-training for months or even years.

Paper Training

To paper train your Mini, select a small, tile-floored room (bathroom, laundry room) where you can confine him. Put your puppy's carrier/bed (door open), water, food, and a few toys in the room. Cover the floor with several layers of newspaper and confine your Mini in the room. When he uses the papers, clean them up and replace them.

After a day or two, leave a corner of the room bare. He'll probably continue using the papers. If he slips up and goes on the bare floor, don't reprimand him unless you see him do it. When your Mini hits the papers every time, gradually reduce the size of the papered area until it's only a three-foot square. Let him use that area until you start taking him outside to relieve himself. At first, you'll have to take him outside frequently. Once he learns to eliminate outside you can stop using the papers.

FEEDING YOUR MINIATURE SCHNAUZER

Food is a big deal to your Miniature Schnauzer. It's not just a source of nutrients, it's a source of fun. Giving your pal nutritious food that tastes good will keep you both happy.

What's What in Dog Food

All dog food contains a mixture of protein, carbohydrates, and fat, as well as essential vitamins and minerals. How these components are combined determines the nutritional balance of the food.

✔ **Protein** is used for the growth and repair of body tissues such as muscles and bones; production of antibodies to fight infection; and production of enzymes and hormones that participate in and regulate bodily functions. Protein can't be stored in the body; excess amounts are converted to fat or eliminated in the urine. Protein sources used in dog foods include meat, dairy products, and soybeans.

✔ **Carbohydrates** provide glucose, the fuel that powers virtually every bodily function from the cellular level to the muscles used when your Mini chases a ball. Excess carbohydrates are stored as glycogen in the liver or muscles, or converted to fat. Carbohydrates are found in cereal grains (for example, rice, corn, or barley) and many other plant sources.

✔ **Fat** is also one of the principal fuels for the body. It's also essential for the production of certain hormones and the proper functioning of some body systems, such as the nervous system. Fat, which is readily stored in the body, is used as a back-up fuel when carbohydrates are unavailable (as in dietary restriction) or metabolically unusable (as in diabetes mellitus). Stored body fat helps maintain body temperature during cold weather. The addition of fat in food improves palatability and increases the calorie content. A variety of plant and animal fats are used in dog foods.

✔ **Vitamins and minerals** are used for a variety of bodily functions, including muscle and nerve function, bone growth and healing, body fluid regulation, and cellular metabolism. You shouldn't need to supplement your Mini's diet with additional vitamins or minerals if you feed a nutritionally complete food, which will contain all the necessary nutrients in the proper proportions. Some vitamins and minerals can be toxic if administered in excessive amounts. Providing vitamins and minerals beyond what your dog needs is also a waste of money as the excess is simply excreted.

Your Mini also needs water, an essential component of every function of the body. Dogs can survive for a long time without eating, but only a short while without water (the body can't store water and only has limited means for conserving it). Your pal needs at least one

TIP

Balancing Act

Dog foods labeled as "complete and balanced" or "nutritionally complete" must meet the nutritional requirements for either adult dogs (adult maintenance) or puppies and pregnant/lactating females (growth and reproduction), set by the Association of American Feed Control Officials. The label must indicate the intended group.

ounce of water per pound of body weight each day, and much more than that in hot weather or during strenuous exercise. In cold weather, you need to make sure your Mini's water doesn't freeze. Dogs can't take in adequate amounts of water by licking ice or eating snow.

Decoding the Label

All dog food labels contain the same information in pretty much the same format. Unfortunately, this doesn't mean that the average person will be able to understand that information. Then again, you don't really have to understand what everything on the label means, because a dog food manufacturer can't claim that its product is nutritionally balanced unless it actually meets certain standards. Not only that, when you read a few labels you'll quickly discover that the nutritional content is pretty much the same for most balanced foods, as long as the foods are the same type (dry, wet, semi-moist, frozen) for the same group (for example, puppies or adults).

First, take a look at the nutritional analysis—the part of the label that tells the protein content, fat content, and so on. The percentages listed represent values of the component on an "as fed" basis, meaning the food just as it comes out of the sack or can, without anything added. Because the companies aren't allowed to list a range of values (such as 20 to 24 percent protein), they list the minimum value ("protein content not less than 20 percent") for protein and fat. This tells you that the percentage of the component might be higher than that, but it isn't less than that. Fiber content is listed as a maximum value ("not more than"). Water content is also listed as a percentage. Carbohydrate content isn't listed, because it's pretty much everything that isn't protein, fat, fiber, or water.

The label lists the percentages in terms of "crude protein" or "crude fat"—the amount of protein or fat analyzed by a machine in a laboratory. Assuming that you're feeding a dog, not a machine, this analysis doesn't tell you much,

because it doesn't measure digestible content—how much of the nutrient your pal can actually use. Manufacturers don't have to provide that information on the label, but you can get more information about it by contacting them (check the label for a phone number or Web site).

The dog food label also contains the ingredient list, which lists the ingredients in descending order by weight.

From the ingredient list, you will be able to determine the major protein source for the food. The primary protein source may be derived from chicken, beef, lamb, or other animals. You may also see some forms of protein that don't sound too appetizing to you. That's okay—your Mini's wild relatives eat a lot of stuff you wouldn't want to find on your dinner table!

You also don't need to worry about grain products (such as corn, wheat, or rice), as long as the food is nutritionally complete. Dogs love meat, but they're actually omnivores (meaning they eat both meat and plant foods) and they need some plant-derived foods for a balanced diet. Wild canidae (wolves, coyotes, and other dog relatives) obtain plant-derived nutrients when they eat herbivorous prey or plants such as fresh green grass (no, it's not because their stomachs are upset).

You'll also find listed in the ingredients any preservatives that have been added to the food. In recent years, owners and experts have questioned the safety of food additives such as BHA, BHT, and ethoxyquin. In response to these concerns, most dog food manufacturers now use a naturally occurring preservative such as mixed tocopherols (vitamin E) and ascorbic acid (vitamin C). Some have eliminated preservatives altogether. Preservative-free foods must be properly stored in a cool, dry environment by

Comparing Dog Foods

To compare the nutritional analyses of different types of food (dry, semimoist, wet, frozen), you need to convert the "as fed" values (the nutritional content of the food with the water included) to "dry matter" values (the nutritional content of the food without the water). To do this, divide the "as fed" value by the proportion of "dry matter" in the food. For example, if a dry food is 10 percent moisture, the "dry matter" is 90 percent or 0.9. Obtain the dry matter values of the other nutrients by dividing the "as fed" values (listed on the label) by 0.9.

both the retailer and the customer to avoid problems with deterioration and rancidity.

Wet, Dry, or In-Between?

In selecting a food for your Mini, you have several choices:

✔ **Dry food** (kibble), which contains the least amount of water, is available in a variety of chunk sizes ranging from about one quarter to three quarters of an inch in diameter. Many dogs find dry food somewhat less appealing than other types, but this varies with the individual. Dry food is bulky and filling. When fed unmoistened, it provides chewing satisfaction and may promote healthy teeth and gums, though some experts debate this. Dry food is relatively inexpensive compared to other foods. It doesn't spoil readily when left in the food dish, so it can be used for free-choice feeding.

✔ **Wet food**, which is available in cans or foil pouches, is relished by most dogs. It's often used to spark the appetite of a finicky eater or a dog that's recovering from an illness. Wet food is more expensive than dry food, but this isn't a problem with small dogs such as MSs. It's easy to store, but the cans or pouches must be refrigerated after opening. Wet food shouldn't be used for free-choice feeding because it spoils rapidly at room temperature.

✔ **Semimoist food**, which is more expensive than either wet or dry food, is easily identified by its resemblance to meat (either ground or chunked). Most dogs love semimoist food. It requires no refrigeration after opening. Unfortunately, much of the storage convenience (and probably palatability) of semimoist food is due to high levels of sugars and preservatives. Because of this, it is not recommended as a primary diet for most dogs.

✔ **Frozen food**, the most expensive of all dog foods, has advantages that are similar to those of wet food. It is available as either cooked or raw products. Frozen food is less convenient than wet food, because it must be thawed before feeding. Unused portions must be refrigerated. Frozen food is not suitable for free-choice feeding.

Switching to Dry Food

If you want to convert your MS from wet, semimoist, or frozen food to dry food, you'll probably have to use the "cold turkey" routine. This doesn't mean that you'll feed your pal nothing but cold turkey, but that you'll feed dry food—and only dry food. If you try to mix the dry food with the usual ration, your buddy will probably just pick her favorite food out of the dish.

At the regular mealtime, put a small amount of dry food (it's okay to moisten it with a little water) in your Mini's dish. Let your pal know that this is dinner (or breakfast). Don't listen to any protests and don't break down and offer anything else.

If your dog refuses to eat, just leave the dish on the floor (don't leave it for more than an hour if you added water because it may get sour).

Be forewarned: you'll need a lot of willpower to resist your friend's attempts to convince you that she'll likely starve if you don't switch back to her favorite food or at least share your dinner! Resist the temptation to offer different food or a between-meal snack. When mealtime rolls around, show your Mini the dish again (or offer fresh water-moistened dry food). Don't worry if she doesn't eat—dogs can go for days without food (that's the usual "meal plan" in the wild). If your little buddy is healthy, she won't starve herself. When she gets hungry enough, she'll eat the dry food. Once that happens, she'll most likely eagerly accept dry food. In fact, you may have to limit the amount you feed, then gradually increase it as her system gets used to the new diet.

TIP

Watch Those Goodies

Too much "people food" can unbalance your Mini's diet, bring on weight problems, and turn her into a finicky eater. Table food, fed as a treat or as part of a meal, shouldn't account for more than 10 percent of your friend's daily caloric intake.

Homemade Food

Some owners choose to forego commercial dog foods altogether, choosing instead to make their own dog food.

Feeding homemade food gives you more control over both the quality and quantity of the ingredients. For example, you can use only "human-quality" ingredients (ingredients you would eat) or avoid ingredients that your Mini doesn't like.

If you make your own dog food, you have the choice of cooking it or leaving it raw, although cooked food is healthier for your Mini. Raw meat may be contaminated with salmonella and *E. coli* bacteria, which can be dangerous for your Mini (and you). Bones—an ingredient often included in raw food recipes—can damage your pal's teeth and digestive tract.

Proponents of homemade dog food contend that it is more easily digested and provides better nutrition than commercial food produced using extrusion (a procedure that combines high heat and pressure). Actually, the effects of extrusion vary. For example, it increases the digestibility of certain nutrients, such as the carbohydrates in grain products. In other cases, most notably with protein and vitamins, extrusion can damage the nutrients, but manufacturers adjust their recipes to compensate for the losses.

When you make homemade food, you can't just throw together a bunch of ingredients. The food needs to provide complete and balanced nutrition, just as a commercial food would. Unfortunately, many recipes for homemade dog food contain no nutritional analysis, so it's impossible to tell if it's providing all the necessary nutrients. If you decide to make homemade food for your Mini, your veterinarian or a veterinary nutritionist can help you find a

recipe that will give your pal all the nutrition she needs.

Feeding Equipment

Your Miniature Schnauzer's food and water dishes don't have to be fancy, just functional, safe, and easy to clean. They can be made of plastic, stainless steel, or crockery. The dishes should be wide-based and heavy, so that they aren't easily tipped over. If your Mini seems especially prone to tipping over her food and water dishes, you can purchase a non-tippable bowl holder at your pet supply store. You can prevent water spillage by providing water in a specially designed bottle that you hang in a holder at an easily accessible height.

At your pet supply store you'll find specialized feeding systems that allow some flexibility in your feeding program. Some of the feeders are designed for free-choice feeding. Others are equipped with a timer and compartments so you can feed specific portions to your Mini even when you're away from home. These gadgets aren't absolutely essential (and certainly won't take the place of proper personal care), but they're convenient.

Feeding Plans

Your Mini's wild relatives eat when food is available, sometimes going for days between meals. Your pal, however, will appreciate regular daily meals. Adult dogs are usually fed once or twice a day. Twice-a-day feeding seems to decrease begging and scavenging behavior. It also decreases the likelihood that your Mini will get overly hungry between meals, bolt her food, and then suffer a digestive upset. Finally, feeding your pal more than once a day will ensure that she gets enough calories to fuel her active lifestyle. Feed your Mini in a quiet place that's away from the household hustle and bustle. If your canine friend sleeps in a carrier or crate, place the food and water dishes close by. Some owners prefer to feed their dogs outside. That's okay too, as long as the feeding spot is sheltered from inclement weather and inaccessible to other dogs. Remember that your pal always needs free access to fresh water, whether she's inside or outside.

Dogs at various life stages and levels of activity have different nutritional requirements. However, to get a general idea of how much to feed, consult the dog food package label. Keep in mind that the company's recommendations are just that—recommendations. Your Miniature Schnauzer may need more or less than the suggested amount.

Free-Choice Feeding

With free-choice feeding, the dog determines when to eat and how much to eat. The owner simply provides an amount of food that exceeds the dog's daily requirement. Free-choice feeding is the simplest feeding plan for the owner. Some dogs adapt readily to this plan, but others tend to overeat and become overweight. This plan also makes it difficult to accurately determine how much the dog is eating. For example, if your Mini loses her appetite because of an illness, you might not detect it until she starts

losing weight. Feeding a puppy free-choice complicates house-training, because the irregular eating schedule makes it difficult to predict when the puppy will need to visit the "potty spot." Free-choice feeding can be used in households with more than one dog, if multiple dishes are provided and an excess of food is always available.

Time-Controlled Feeding

With time-controlled feeding, the owner offers a surplus of food and the dog eats as much as it wants in a predetermined time period, usually 15 to 20 minutes. This feeding plan allows the dog to self-regulate its food intake over a much shorter period of time.

Overeating is less of a problem with dogs on a time-controlled feeding plan than with those that are fed free-choice. It's also easier to determine whether the dog is eating. Because of the regular meal schedule, time-controlled feeding makes it easier to anticipate a puppy's house-training needs.

Portion-Controlled Feeding

With portion-controlled feeding, the owner offers a predetermined amount of food (one meal's worth) and the dog decides when and how much to eat. For example, if you feed your Mini twice a day, you would give it half of the total daily amount in the morning and half in the evening. Portion-controlled feeding affords the dog owner the greatest amount of control with respect to quantity eaten. Any increase or decrease in food intake can be detected immediately. This plan is not suitable for households with more than one dog. It makes house-training more difficult because the puppy can eat throughout the day.

Macro Minis

Obesity is the number one nutrition-related health problem in dogs. In the majority of cases, the cause is twofold: too much food—dog food, snacks, treats, and "people food"—and not enough exercise.

Obesity increases your Mini's risk of developing serious health problems such as diabetes, liver disease, or pancreatitis. It can aggravate orthopedic problems such as patellar luxation and hip dysplasia. Obesity can force your buddy's heart to work harder and make breathing more difficult, even at rest. These problems can seriously impair your Mini's ability to run, play, or even walk, which of course will increase the probability of continued weight problems.

As most people know from personal experience, the best time to fight the battle of the bulge is before it starts. Don't overfeed your Mini. Limit between-meal treats, or, if you simply can't resist, give her low-calorie goodies such as fresh or frozen veggies. Make sure she gets plenty of exercise—every day. If she can't

exercise vigorously because of health problems, ask your veterinarian to recommend an exercise program.

If your Mini is seriously overweight or obese, it's time for more drastic action. Consult your veterinarian about a comprehensive weight-loss program, which should include a complete checkup, diet plan, and exercise recommendations. Your veterinarian may advise feeding your pal a prescription food specifically formulated for weight loss. These foods, which are available only from veterinarians, are more effective than non-prescription "light" or "reduced calorie" foods for major weight loss.

What *Not* to Feed

So far, we've talked a lot about what to feed your Miniature Schnauzer. Here are some things to avoid:

✔ **Bones.** Feeding your Mini raw or cooked bones can put him at risk for digestive tract injury (perforation or obstruction), constipation, and tooth fractures. Raw bones may also be contaminated with harmful bacteria such as salmonella or *E. coli*. Partially chewed bones (raw or cooked) also foster the growth of bacteria. If your MS likes to chew—and most dogs do—give him a nylon bone or one of the many dog-safe chew toys available at your pet supply store.

✔ **Raw meat.** Uncooked meat may contain *Salmonella* or *E. coli*, which can be dangerous for your Mini—and you.

✔ **Raw eggs.** Raw egg whites contain avidin, an enzyme that blocks the uptake of biotin, an important B vitamin. Raw eggs may also contain *Salmonella*.

✔ **Chocolate and other kinds of candy.** Did you ever hear of a wolf or coyote eating a

---

Weight Check

What's a normal weight? You should be able to just feel your Mini's ribs. She should also have a "waist" that's visible from the top or side. If you've been feeding the recommended amount of food and your friend seems to be losing weight, increase the amount, perhaps by increasing the number of feedings per day. If she's gaining too much weight, cut back on the amount you feed.

Note: *Consult your veterinarian if your Mini's weight loss or gain is excessive or persistent or is accompanied by signs of illness.*

candy bar? Dogs don't need sweets and they don't need the dental problems that go with them. Chocolate is especially dangerous because it contains methylxanthines, caffeine-like substances that can be toxic to dogs. If you want to treat your Mini, give her a dog biscuit or bit of fresh veggie instead.

✔ **Grapes and raisins.** Dogs have suffered renal failure after eating grapes and raisins. The toxic dose varies; some dogs are more sensitive than others.

✔ **Onions, garlic, and related foods.** If eaten in sufficient quantity, these foods can cause digestive tract irritation and anemia. The toxic dose varies, depending on the ingredient (for example, onions are more toxic than garlic) and the size of the dog.

✔ **Yeasted bread dough.** This food can actually rise in the digestive tract, causing obstruction. It also produces alcohol as it rises.

✔ **Macadamia nuts.** These tasty nuts can make your Mini sick. Symptoms include vomiting, weakness, and incoordination.

✔ **Avocados.** You may like them on your salad, but avocados can cause vomiting and diarrhea if your Mini eats enough of them.

✔ **Alcohol.** Many owners who wouldn't dream of offering alcohol to a child think it's okay to

TIP

Dietary Extras

If you feed your youngster a nutritionally balanced puppy food, you don't need to add meat, milk, eggs, or any type of supplement. Dietary additions could even harm your Mini by unbalancing that already-balanced food.

coax their dog into taking a sip or two, or even more. Dogs are extremely sensitive to the effects of alcohol. Because of the size difference, a small drink for a person is a huge amount for most dogs. A drunk dog isn't funny, it's a medical emergency.

✔ **"Recreational" drugs.** Like alcohol, these substances can have profound and disastrous effects on dogs.

Minis with Special Dietary Needs

Miniature Schnauzer puppies, seniors, and those with certain health problems have special nutritional requirements.

Puppies

Puppies have a higher metabolic rate than adult dogs, so they require more calories per pound of body weight. They also need comparatively more protein because they're growing and developing so rapidly. To meet these needs, completely balanced puppy foods contain greater amounts of protein and fat than adult foods. They also contain the correct amount and balance of vitamins and minerals such as calcium and phosphorus, which puppies need for proper bone development and growth. Some puppy foods also supply other nonessential nutrients—for example, docosohexaenoic acid (DHA), an omega fatty acid that is thought to optimize brain development and learning in puppies.

Pudgy puppies are cute, but your baby Mini will be healthier—as a puppy and throughout her life—if you keep her on the slender side. Puppyhood obesity may cause abnormal skeletal development and accelerate the onset of clinical symptoms of patellar luxation and other inherited orthopedic problems. An obese puppy is more likely to grow into an obese adult, at risk for serious illnesses such as pancreatitis and diabetes mellitus.

If your Mini puppy has just been weaned, she'll need to eat at least four times a day because it's difficult, if not impossible, for these little ones to get all the nutrients they need when fed less often.

When your puppy is about 10 to 12 weeks old, decrease the number of feedings to three a day. You'll need to increase the total daily intake of food as your puppy grows. When she's about six months old, decrease the number of feedings to the adult schedule of two times a day.

When your Mini is about a year old, she'll be ready for adult food. Making the change gradually will keep her from experiencing any digestive upset. On the first day, substitute adult food for one-fourth of her puppy food. On the second day, feed her a half-and-half mixture of puppy food and adult food. On the third day, substitute adult food for three-fourths of her puppy food. On the fourth day, feed her only the adult food.

Senior Minis

Nutrition for the senior dog is complicated because it depends on the individual dog's overall health, body condition, and ongoing health problems, if any.

Keeping your senior Mini at the proper weight (not too fat and not too thin) is especially important because it can be difficult to change an older dog's body condition. Dogs, like many people, tend to become less active as they age. When this is added to an age-related decrease in metabolic rate, the result is often substantial weight gain. To keep your older friend from becoming too fat, you'll need to decrease the amount of calories she eats and/or increase her activity level. For example, you might switch her to a dog food specially formulated to meet the needs of senior dogs. These foods contain less fat and fewer calories than standard adult foods, with added fiber to promote a feeling of fullness. You can also try to get your Mini to move around a bit more—for example, by taking her out for a daily 20-minute walk. If your pal has health problems, be sure to get your veterinarian's okay before starting an exercise program.

Some older dogs have the opposite weight problem: they're too thin. A senior Mini may lose weight if she has a chronic health problem (such as dental problems, cancer, or heart disease) that decreases her appetite. She may not be able to smell or taste food very well—a dog seldom eats what it can't smell or taste. Sometimes the problem is caused by inefficient digestion or absorption of nutrients; the dog eats normal (or even increased) amounts, but can't acquire the necessary nutrients. If your senior Mini is underweight, she may benefit from food fortified with high-quality fat, which will make the food more palatable and increase its calorie content. If she's underweight because of a chronic health problem, your veterinarian may switch her to a prescription food as an adjunct to medical treatment.

At one time, it was thought that senior dogs needed less protein than younger dogs, principally to spare the kidneys, which function less efficiently with age. It's now known that protein metabolism decreases with age and senior dogs actually need more protein, not less, than younger adults. If your senior Mini doesn't get enough protein, she could experience weakness,

loss of muscle mass, and impairment of her immune system. To prevent these problems, feed your pal a nutritionally balanced senior food; most now contain as much protein as puppy foods (check the label to be sure).

Dogs with Health Problems

Special diets can be useful adjuncts in the medical management of dogs with certain health problems, such as kidney disease, heart disease, liver disease, and food allergies. Your veterinarian may also recommend a special diet if your Mini develops pancreatitis. Dogs that are recovering from major illness or surgery can benefit from a diet that is specially formulated to provide maximal nutrition with easy digestibility. Unlike regular dog food, special diets are available only from your veterinarian, who can advise you about their usefulness in the management of your friend's health problem.

A healthy Miniature Schnauzer is easy to spot. Looking good from nose to tail, this is a dog that's alert, animated, and interested in everything. In appearance and action, a healthy Mini says to the world, "I feel great!"

Your Veterinarian

Proper veterinary care is essential for maintaining your Miniature Schnauzer's health. In addition to providing medical care, your veterinarian can answer your questions about behavior, breeding, and nutrition. Don't be tempted to seek veterinary care and advice from neighbors, breeders, or pet store personnel, or to just do it yourself. There's no substitute for professional veterinary care.

As veterinary medicine has become more sophisticated and more specialized, choosing a veterinarian has become more complex. There are now veterinarians who specialize with respect to species—treating, for instance, only dogs and cats—and veterinarians who limit their practice to a clinical specialty, such as surgery. You will probably want to take your Mini to a veterinarian who deals primarily with companion animals (also called small animals—mostly dogs and cats).

Take the time to find a veterinarian who's just right for your Miniature Schnauzer (and you).

✔ Check with the breeder or former owner of your Mini.

✔ Ask your dog-owning friends which veterinarian they use.

✔ Contact a nearby school of veterinary medicine (there are more than 30 in North America); they may have a list of veterinarians in your area.

✔ If you're moving, ask your current veterinarian to recommend one in your new location.

✔ Check the Internet. The American Animal Hospital Association, an organization of veterinarians, has a locating service on its Web site (*www.healthypet.org*).

Once you've gotten the names of two or three veterinarians, arrange to interview them. During the visit, observe how the veterinarian and staff get along with the patients and their owners. Tour the hospital, if possible. Take your

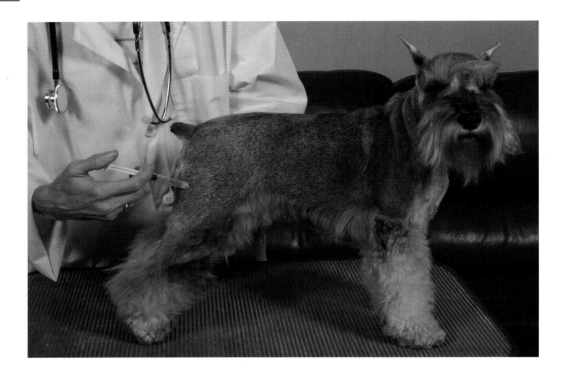

time and ask a lot of questions; a good veterinarian will be happy to answer them.

Vaccinations

Vaccinations can protect your Mini from many diseases. All dogs need vaccinations for rabies, distemper, infectious hepatitis, and parvovirus infection because these diseases are highly contagious and difficult to treat. Only dogs at high risk of exposure need vaccinations for diseases such as leptospirosis, kennel cough, and Lyme disease, which are usually less serious and easier to treat. For example, a show dog may need vaccination against kennel cough in addition to the core vaccinations. Your

veterinarian can tell you what vaccinations your Mini needs.

Rabies

Rabies is a viral disease that can affect any warm-blooded mammal. It is most commonly contracted when saliva from an infected animal enters an open wound (usually a bite wound) and comes into contact with nerve endings. A dog with rabies may first demonstrate an unusual change in behavior. For instance, a previously shy dog may become friendly, while a good-natured dog may become nervous and reclusive. In the second stage of rabies, the dog becomes excitable and hyperreactive (the origin of the term "mad dog"). The dog may become

Core Vaccinations

Disease	Initial Vaccination Series			Boosters	
	Start (age)	Revaccination	Until (age)	First (age)	Subsequent
Distemper*	6–8 wks	every 3–4 wks	16 wks	1 yr	every 3 yrs
Hepatitis*	6–8 wks	every 3–4 wks	16 wks	1 yr	every 3 yrs
Parvovirus*	6–8 wks	every 3–4 wks	18–20 wks	1 yr	every 3 yrs
Rabies	16 wks	none		1 yr	every 1 or 3 yrs**

*Dogs older than 16 weeks when initially vaccinated need only one revaccination 3–4 weeks later, then boosters as shown.
**Depends on local law.

aggressive and attempt to bite inanimate or even imaginary objects. Some dogs react differently and become stuporous and oblivious to their surroundings. During the final stage of rabies, the dog becomes progressively paralyzed. Drooling (foaming at the mouth) occurs because paralysis of the jaw muscles makes it difficult to swallow. Death usually occurs within 24 to 48 hours.

Distemper

Canine distemper is a highly contagious viral disease that is spread primarily via body secretions (urine, feces, saliva, nasal discharge) and by contact with contaminated objects such as

Success Story

Pets were once the principal means of transmission of rabies to humans, but vaccination of dogs and cats has markedly decreased the incidence of human rabies. Wild animals such as skunks and opossums are now a much greater threat—to humans and pets.

brushes, blankets, and food bowls. The incubation period for distemper is 14 to 18 days. Young dogs that have not been immunized are highly susceptible.

A dog with distemper may at first have mild cold-like symptoms: low-grade fever, nasal discharge, and listlessness. As the disease progresses, the dog develops a puslike discharge from the eyes and nose, along with other symptoms such as anorexia, vomiting, diarrhea, and coughing. In the later stages of distemper, the dog may show signs of acute encephalitis: seizures, muscle twitching, incoordination, crying out, fearful behavior, circling, and blindness. The more severe the neurological problems are, the poorer the outlook for recovery. Dogs that recover from distemper may have permanent neurological problems such as involuntary muscle spasms and impaired vision.

Hepatitis

Infectious canine hepatitis, a viral disease, most often occurs in young dogs. Most infections are inapparent, but occasionally the virus

Vaccination Reactions

Your Mini puppy may be a little "under the weather" for about 24 hours after vaccination, with a low-grade fever, listlessness, and loss of appetite. Usually no treatment is needed, beyond sympathy and extra cuddles, but contact your veterinarian if your little friend develops other symptoms such as hives, itchiness, diarrhea, or difficulty breathing, which could mean a more serious reaction.

causes a rapidly progressing disease that resembles distemper and parvovirus infection. Infected dogs shed the virus in all bodily secretions, including feces, urine, nasal secretions, saliva, and blood. Dogs become infected by inhaling or ingesting the virus. The incubation period for hepatitis is four to seven days.

Initially, the dog with hepatitis may have a rather high fever (103 to 106°F [39–41°C]), which decreases within 24 hours. In mild cases, the dog recovers after one or two days. In moderate cases, the temperature fails to return to normal and increases again in one or two days. The dog often becomes lethargic and anorexic. Other signs of severe hepatitis include small pinpoint hemorrhages (visible on the gums), vomiting and bloody diarrhea, as well as abdominal tenderness and distension. In some dogs, coughing develops and progresses to pneumonia. When hepatitis affects multiple body systems, the prognosis is grim: the dog may lapse into a coma and die, or may die from shock.

Parvovirus

Parvovirus infections are often inapparent, but factors such as young age, stress, intestinal parasites, or bacterial infection may predispose a dog to severe disease. The principal signs of parvovirus infection are vomiting, diarrhea, lethargy, and anorexia. Severely affected dogs can develop persistent vomiting and severe bloody diarrhea, which can lead to death in less than 24 hours. Young puppies infected with parvovirus sometimes develop myocarditis (inflammation of the heart). A dog that has recovered from parvovirus infection will have lifelong immunity.

Noncore Vaccinations

Leptospirosis

Leptospirosis is caused by a spiral-shaped bacteria called a spirochete. The organism is shed in the urine, which contaminates soil, water, and feed. Dogs become infected when they come into contact with infected urine or contaminated substances.

Leptospirosis initially causes fever, vomiting, and loss of appetite. Jaundice occurs in some dogs, causing a yellowish coloration of the sclera (whites of the eyes), conjunctiva (linings of the eyelids), and mouth. Dogs that have recovered from leptospirosis can shed the infective organism for up to four years.

Vaccination for leptospirosis doesn't provide complete immunity because the vaccine protects only against the most common strains of the bacteria that cause the disease, rather than all of them. In addition, for unknown reasons, some dogs fail to respond to the vaccine.

Kennel Cough

Kennel cough (infectious tracheobronchitis) is a highly-contagious disease caused by several different organisms, including bacteria (especially *Bordetella bronchiseptica*) and viruses (parain-fluenza virus, adenovirus-2). It is usually a mild, self-limiting disease.

Infected dogs have mild to severe recurrent episodes of coughing, which may be aggravated by exercise, excitement, or pressure on the tra-chea. The cough may sound soft and moist, or harsh and dry. Infected dogs often gag at the end of a coughing episode, which sometimes leads owners to mistakenly believe that their dog is vomiting. Most dogs with kennel cough are active and alert, with a normal appetite and no fever. In rare cases—primarily in immunocompromised adults and unvaccinated puppies—the disease can cause fever, pneumonia, and death.

Recovery from kennel cough usually takes about two to three weeks. Recovered dogs may shed infective organisms for more than three months. Some dogs become persistently infected carriers.

Vaccination against kennel cough will not completely prevent infection, but it will decrease the incidence and severity of the disease.

Lyme Disease

Lyme disease is caused by *Borrelia burgdor-feri*, an organism carried by deer ticks. The disease, which may occur months after the infective tick bite, causes fever, weakness, joint pain, and lameness. The lameness may be transient, recurring at intervals as short as one month and as long as 23 months. If left untreated, Lyme disease can cause serious complications and even death.

Deer ticks are found primarily on certain species of deer and mice. The tick must feed for about 48 hours on the dog in order to cause infection. Lyme disease has been reported in nearly every state in the United States, but the incidence is highest on the Atlantic and Pacific coasts and the upper Midwest.

Lyme disease can be treated successfully with antibiotics. Immunization against the disease provides only limited protection and is most effective in dogs that have not been previously exposed to infected ticks.

Spaying and Neutering

Spaying or neutering your Mini is an important step that you can take toward reducing the number of unwanted dogs. Each day, thousands of healthy but unwanted puppies and dogs die because there are no homes for them. Responsible owners control their dog's reproductive potential. Spaying or neutering is an easy way to accomplish this.

Spaying (ovariohysterectomy) is surgical removal of the ovaries and uterus. Neutering is surgical removal of the testicles (castration) or sterilization by testicular injection of a chemical compound. Puppies can be spayed or surgically neutered when they're eight weeks old, but many veterinarians recommend waiting until the age of four to six months. Chemical neutering is

TIP

Tiny Ticks

Not every tiny tick is a deer tick; some are "seed ticks," immature forms of other types of ticks.

performed only between the ages of three and ten months.

Spaying and surgical neutering provide benefits other than limiting reproduction. These procedures often decrease roaming, lessening exposure to dangers such as cars, sick or aggressive dogs, and toxins. Surgical neutering also reduces or eliminates the occurrence of certain diseases of the prostate and testicles. (Chemical neutering doesn't completely eliminate testosterone production, so it doesn't provide the same benefits as surgical neutering.) Spayed females don't come into "heat" (estrus), so there's no bloody discharge to stain your carpet or furniture and no amorous male dogs hanging around. Spaying also decreases the occurrence of mammary cancer (if the dog is spayed before her first estrus) and eliminates uterine infections.

Contrary to what you might have heard, spaying or neutering will not change your Mini's basic personality, unless you consider elimination of canine romantic tendencies a personality change! Nor will these procedures necessarily cause obesity, unless your pal gets too many treats and not enough exercise.

Signs of Illness and Injury

Recognizing some of the more common signs of illness will help you determine when your Miniature Schnauzer needs veterinary care.

✔ Unusual behavior (listlessness, disinterest in surroundings, irritability, hyperactivity, seizures. Contact your veterinarian immediately if your Mini is unconscious or has a seizure.

✔ Difficulty standing or moving around (incoordination, stumbling, circling, limping, paralysis). Contact your veterinarian immediately if your Mini appears to be paralyzed.

✔ Pain (persistent whining, growling, or aggression when handled, reluctance to move, limping, hiding).

✔ Obvious wound or injury (cuts, puncture wounds, abscesses, broken bones). Contact your veterinarian immediately if your Mini is bleeding uncontrollably or appears to have a broken bone.

✔ Change in eating or drinking behavior (not eating, not drinking, eating more than usual, excessive thirst).

✔ Respiratory abnormality (coughing, sneezing, labored breathing, gasping). Contact your veterinarian immediately if your Mini's tongue or gums look blue, or he collapses.

✔ Digestive tract abnormality (vomiting, diarrhea, constipation).

✔ Urinary tract abnormality (blood in the urine, absence of urination, excessive urination, straining to urinate, house-training "accidents," especially in a well-house-trained dog). Contact your veterinarian immediately if your Mini cannot urinate.

✔ Secretion or discharge from nose, eyes, mouth, or elsewhere (mucus, watery fluid, pus, blood, or other secretions). Normal secretions such as tears and nasal mucus are usually unnoticeable in healthy dogs.

✔ Weight loss. Unexplained weight loss (unrelated to a decrease in amount fed or increased activity) accompanies disorders such as internal parasites, diabetes, cancer, and many others.

✔ Fever. Normal canine body temperature: 100.5 to 102.5°F (38.1 to 39.2°C). Excitement or excessive activity can elevate body temperature.

Note: Trust your own judgment: if your Mini just doesn't seem to be "acting right," contact your veterinarian or emergency clinic to find out if he needs medical attention.

Specific Problems

Cuts and Bleeding

Cuts (lacerations) range in severity from minor to life-threatening. Most cuts are minor, but even a minor cut can seem serious, because a small amount of blood can look like a lot, especially if it gets smeared. Blood from a vein is dark red and flows in a steady stream. Blood from an artery is bright red and spurts. Arterial bleeding is usually more serious than venous bleeding. To stop bleeding, apply gentle but firm pressure directly to the wound with a gauze pad, clean cloth, or towel. It's okay to tape the gauze or cloth over the wound, but don't use a tourniquet, which can cause pain and tissue damage if it's not used correctly.

Vomiting and Diarrhea

If your Mini vomits once, you probably don't need to be alarmed, especially if he doesn't have any other signs of illness. Many dogs vomit occasionally, especially after eating grass or a very large meal. An isolated episode of diarrhea is also not unusual, especially if your MS is nervous or has increased his water consumption due to hot weather. Repeated vomiting or diarrhea, however, could mean your pal has a more serious problem such as gastroenteritis, pancreatitis, or a gastrointestinal foreign body or other obstruction. Electrolytes, which are essential components of many chemical reactions in the body, are lost during vomiting and diarrhea. Dehydration may also occur with repeated episodes. Young puppies are particularly prone to becoming dehydrated by persistent vomiting and diarrhea.

If your Mini vomits or has diarrhea three or more times in 24 hours, he needs to be checked by your veterinarian as soon as possible. Do not administer any medications unless directed to do so by your veterinarian.

Fractures (Broken Bones)

A closed (simple) fracture is one without an open wound. An open (compound) fracture is one in which an open would occurs. Open fractures are more serious because the risk of infection is greater.

You might not be able to tell if your Mini has a fracture just by looking, especially if the fracture involves his feet, ribs, or head. If he's broken his leg, however, it will probably be so painful

TIP

Safety First

Since most broken bones occur when a dog is hit by a car, keeping your Miniature Schnauzer in a fenced yard or on a leash will help prevent this injury.

that he won't want to bear any weight on it at all. The leg may dangle oddly or appear to have an extra joint.

If you think your Mini has a broken bone, you should take him to your veterinarian or emergency clinic as soon as possible. Don't attempt to bandage or splint the injury. Move him gently and carefully to minimize movement of the broken bone. If he reacts violently to the pain, you may need to muzzle him to avoid being bitten.

Eye Problems

The eye is a very delicate structure that can be seriously damaged by disease or trauma. Some eye problems, such as conjunctivitis, corneal injuries, cataracts, and glaucoma, are more commonly encountered than others.

Foreign bodies: Grass, seeds, splinters, or other foreign bodies in your Mini's eye may or may not cause discomfort, depending on the location of the object and whether it is embedded in the eye or surrounding structures. Tearing, squinting, or holding the lid tightly shut, and nervousness about being touched near the eye are all signs that indicate ocular (eye) pain.

If you think your Mini has an ocular foreign body, gently pry his lids apart and carefully examine the eye. You may need to muzzle him and/or have someone hold him while you do this. Taking care not to touch the eye, gently flood it with warm water or eye irrigating solution (such as Dacriose or Eye-Stream, available at your pharmacy) dripped from a cotton ball. Repeat, if necessary. Use only this flooding technique—do not try to remove the foreign body with a cotton swab, gauze pad, or tissue. If you can't wash the object out of the eye, take your Miniature Schnauzer to your veterinarian as soon as possible.

Conjunctivitis: Conjunctivitis is an inflammation of the lining of the eyelids (the conjunctiva) that can be caused by local or generalized infection or by contact with irritating substances. If your pal has conjunctivitis, his conjunctiva will be red and inflamed. Depending on the cause of the problem, he may have excessive tearing or a mucus-like discharge from the affected eye(s). The pain associated with conjunctivitis varies.

Corneal injuries: Corneal injuries occur when the cornea—the clear outer covering of the eye—has been scratched or punctured. If your Mini has a corneal injury, he may vigorously resist your attempts to examine his eye. These injuries are often extremely painful. Excessive tearing may occur. Some corneal injuries cannot be detected without special diagnostic techniques. In other cases, the cornea may appear cloudy over the injury.

Cataracts: A cataract is a cloudiness of the lens of the eye. If your Miniature Schnauzer has a cataract, you may be able to see the cloudiness when you look directly into the eye. Severe cataracts can cause blindness. In some cases, surgical removal of the affected lens can restore vision, at least partially. Many older dogs develop senile cataracts, which are not as serious as cataracts in younger dogs. Senile cataracts are not usually treated.

Glaucoma: Glaucoma is a disease that causes excessive pressure within the eyeball. The increased pressure eventually damages the structure of the eye, causing blindness. Glaucoma can sometimes be treated successfully with medication. In advanced cases, removal of the eye may be necessary.

If your Mini has an eye problem, even if it seems to be minor, he should be evaluated by your veterinarian. Prompt treatment may save his sight. Other than flooding the eye to remove minor foreign bodies, never attempt any type of home treatment for an eye problem unless directed to do so by your veterinarian.

Ear Problems

The most common ear problem encountered in dogs is otitis externa, an inflammation of the external ear canal. Otitis externa has many causes: foreign bodies (for example, foxtails, grass awns), ear mites, irritation, and excessive moisture. Allergies, to food or inhaled substances, are a common, but often overlooked, cause. Secondary bacterial or yeast infections often complicate otitis externa. If your Mini develops otitis externa, he may repeatedly shake his head or scratch the affected ear, which may have a discharge and bad smell.

As soon as you notice these symptoms, take your pal to your veterinarian for diagnosis and treatment. Left untreated, the infection/inflammation can spread to the middle ear or inner ear and cause very serious complications.

Heart Disease

Heart disease may be congenital (present at birth) or acquired (developed after birth). Congenital heart diseases are often characterized by structural abnormalities, such as defects between adjacent chambers of the heart, or malpositioning of the vessels around the heart. A few of these abnormalities can be corrected surgically. Acquired heart disease takes many forms; one of the most common acquired heart diseases is mitral insufficiency, in which one of the heart valves does not close properly and allows some of the blood to flow backward instead of forward. Many cases of mitral

insufficiency can be well managed with proper medication.

Some Miniature Schnauzers have a heart disease called sick sinus syndrome, which occurs when the sinoatrial node (the heart's "pacemaker") doesn't work properly. This causes a very slow, irregular heart rate that doesn't increase when it should, such as during exercise. Dogs with sick sinus syndrome often have episodes of fainting, because the slow heart rate deprives the brain of blood (and oxygen). Sick sinus syndrome can be successfully treated by implantation of a cardiac pacemaker (identical to those used in humans).

The symptoms of heart disease, which vary depending on the specific condition and its severity, often include lethargy, shortness of breath, coughing, abdominal distension, and exercise intolerance.

Pancreatitis

Pancreatitis is an inflammation of the pancreas, an organ that secretes enzymes that help digest food. The cause of pancreatitis is often not known, but eating large quantities of high-fat food is thought to be a significant factor. Many dogs that develop pancreatitis are obese. Some Miniature Schnauzers are afflicted with a condition known as idiopathic hyperlipoproteinemia, an abnormality of fat and protein metabolism that may increase the incidence of pancreatitis.

Pancreatitis usually causes depression, loss of appetite, and vomiting. Severe abdominal pain is often present, and the dog may cry out when its abdomen is touched. Some dogs periodically assume an unusual stance ("praying position") in which the front legs and chest are lowered to the floor while the hindlimbs are maintained in a standing position.

Mild cases of pancreatitis may spontaneously resolve. Treatment of more severe cases involves withholding food, along with intravenous fluid therapy and other supportive care. Avoiding high-fat meals can help prevent recurrence of pancreatitis. In some cases of chronic pancreatitis, the fat content of the diet must be severely restricted.

Skin Problems

Skin problems have many causes, including external parasites (fleas, ticks, and mites), allergies, endocrine diseases, and bacterial and yeast/fungal infections. Depending on the condition, the skin may be dry and scaly or moist and oozing. The problem may be generalized, as with allergies, or localized, as with fungal infections such as ringworm. Itching (pruritus), which may be severe, occurs with many skin problems. The resulting self-trauma increases the likelihood of secondary bacterial or yeast

infections. Hair loss, when present, may be limited to a certain area or occur all over the body. If your Mini develops a skin problem that's more than an uncomplicated case of fleas or ticks, don't try to treat it yourself. Given the diversity of skin problems and the high incidence of secondary infections, it's important to rely on your veterinarian to diagnose the problem(s) and prescribe appropriate treatment.

Cancer

Nearly half of all dogs over the age of ten die from cancer. The disease can take many forms. Some types of cancer are easy to see and look like nodules or sores. Some can only be detected with special diagnostic techniques. Sometimes cancer causes symptoms that mimic another disease.

The outlook for a dog with cancer varies, depending on the type and size of tumor, the duration of illness, whether it has spread to other areas of the body, and the treatment chosen. Much progress has been made in the treatment of cancer in animals. Treatment options include surgical removal, chemotherapy, or radiation therapy. These treatments are often combined to produce a higher rate of remission or cure.

Poisoning

Substances that are poisonous to your Mini range from seemingly innocuous compounds such as chocolate to more obvious poisons such as strychnine. Most poisonings occur when a dog ingests a toxic substance; but poisoning can also occur by skin contact or inhalation.

Symptoms of poisoning vary widely because of the great diversity of toxic substances. Some poisons cause vomiting; others do not. A dog that has been poisoned may be lethargic or even comatose, or may be restless or agitated. Progressively severe seizures may occur with some poisons.

Sometimes other diseases cause signs that are similar to those of poisoning.

If you think your Mini has been poisoned, contact your veterinarian or emergency clinic immediately. If you can identify the poison, tell your veterinarian, and provide any label or container information, if available. Do not give your pal any treatment or medication unless instructed to do so by your veterinarian.

Heatstroke

Dogs cool off by panting, which is a less efficient method of temperature control than sweating. Heatstroke occurs when a dog cannot get rid of excess body heat. Predisposing factors include a heavy coat, obesity, excessive activity, and confinement in a poorly ventilated, warm environment.

One of the most common causes of heatstroke in dogs is confinement in a car on a warm day. *Never* leave your Mini in a closed car, even on a mild day; the temperature in the car can quickly become dangerously high.

A dog with heatstroke will be depressed and lethargic. The body temperature will be extremely high, sometimes as high as 106°F (41.1°C). The dog may actually feel hot to the touch, especially on the ears or in the mouth. Signs of shock—high heart rate, high respiratory rate, pale gums, and collapse—may be present.

Since heatstroke can be fatal, immediate veterinary care is necessary. Emergency procedures to help lower body temperature include wetting down the fur with cool (not cold) water, placing ice packs (wrapped in a washcloth) in the groin area, and offering cold water or ice chips, if the dog is conscious.

Internal Parasites

Roundworms

Roundworms (ascarids) are the most common canine internal parasite. Dogs of all ages can become infected when they ingest roundworm eggs, found mainly in the soil. In puppies, roundworm larvae migrate to the lungs, where they are coughed up and swallowed. They then pass into the small intestine to develop into adults. In adult dogs, the larvae migrate to other body tissues, such as the muscles, where they become dormant. Pregnancy activates the dormant larvae, which migrate to the placenta or mammary gland to infect the puppies prior to birth or when they nurse.

Heavy roundworm infection in young puppies can cause abdominal pain and distension, diarrhea, stunted growth, and dull hair coat. Severely infected puppies may develop pneumonia as the larvae migrate through the lungs. Roundworm infection is usually asymptomatic in adult dogs.

Medication for roundworm infestation is usually quite safe and can be administered to puppies as young as two weeks of age. More than one treatment is often necessary to completely eliminate the parasites. Effective control of roundworms in adult dogs, especially breeding females, and in the environment decreases the severity of infestations in young puppies.

Hookworms

Hookworms are bloodsucking intestinal parasites that are found in dogs of all ages. Infection

TIP

Health Threat

Roundworms and hookworms are public health problems. Roundworm larvae can infect humans and migrate through the body (visceral larval migrans) or eye (ocular larval migrans). Some types of hookworm larvae migrate under the skin (cutaneous larval migrans) or into the intestines (eosinophilic enteritis).

most commonly occurs when infective larvae are ingested or penetrate the skin. Puppies can become infected prior to birth or while nursing if the mother has hookworm larvae migrating within her body. Hookworms develop rapidly in the body and eggs are passed in the feces after two to three weeks. The larvae can survive for three to four months in the environment.

Clinical signs of hookworm infection include diarrhea (sometimes bloody or tarry), pale gums, anemia, weakness, and weight loss. Severely affected puppies may need blood transfusions.

Regular treatment of adults and puppies will decrease the incidence of hookworm infection. Some medications are safe for puppies as young as two weeks of age.

As with most intestinal parasites, control of hookworms is facilitated by good sanitation and the use of impervious flooring in kennels and runs.

Whipworms

Whipworms are commonly found in the colon and cecum of dogs of all ages. Infection occurs when infective eggs are ingested. Most whipworm infections are asymptomatic, but some dogs may develop chronic or intermittent diarrhea. Because female whipworms shed eggs sporadically, several fecal examinations may be needed to diagnose the infection. Whipworm eggs are very resistant in the environment and frequent treatment of runs and kennels may be necessary to prevent reinfection.

Tapeworms

The most common type of tapeworm infection in dogs occurs when infected intermediate hosts—fleas and lice—are ingested. A less common species of tapeworm is carried by rodents, rabbits, sheep, and cattle. Tapeworms cause few symptoms in dogs, but some may experience a slight decline in body condition. Intact tapeworms are long and flat, with a body that is divided into infective segments called proglottids, which are shed in the feces. Owners often see the mobile, rice-sized proglottids in their dog's anal area or feces. Treatment of tapeworm infection involves eliminating both the parasites and the intermediate hosts. Thus, flea and lice control and elimination of scavenging and hunting behaviors are important aspects of effective treatment.

Coccidia

The term *coccidia* does not refer to a single parasite, but rather to any of a group of six protozoan parasites. Infection occurs by ingestion of infective egg-packets (oocysts) or infective cyst-containing tissues from a transport host, such as rodents and other prey.

Coccidia infection usually causes no clinical signs, especially in healthy adult dogs. Factors such as young age, concurrent disease, stress, malnutrition, poor sanitation, and overcrowding can predispose a dog to clinical disease from coccidiosis.

The major clinical sign of coccidiosis is diarrhea, but vomiting, listlessness, weight loss, and dehydration can also occur. If clinical signs are present, treatment is indicated, expecially in newborn puppies. Healthy dogs with asymptomatic infections may not need treatment.

Heartworms

Heartworms live in the heart and in some of the large blood vessels around the heart. This parasite, which is spread by mosquitoes, occurs throughout the United States. The cycle starts when a female mosquito ingests immature infective heartworms (microfilariae) while feeding on an infected dog. The microfilariae develop within the mosquito, which eventually introduces them into another dog while feeding. After migrating through the dog's body, the young adult heartworms enter the blood vessels and travel to arteries within the lungs. There they develop further and begin producing microfilariae. The entire cycle takes about six months.

At first, adult heartworms live only in the vessels of the lungs, but as they multiply, they invade the vessels between the heart and the lungs, and eventually the heart itself.

Many cases of heartworm infection are asymptomatic, especially in the early stages or in sedentary dogs. As the disease progresses, coughing, shortness of breath, and exercise intolerance occur. Severe heartworm infection can eventually cause heart failure and death.

Heartworm infections must be treated with two types of medication—one to kill the adult heartworms and another to kill the microfilariae. Treatment can be risky, because the dead and disintegrating heartworms can cause pul-

monary embolism if they lodge in the small blood vessels of the lungs. (Specialized blood cells eventually clean up the dead heartworms, but it takes several weeks.)

It's much easier to prevent heartworm disease than to cure it once it has developed. Monthly treatment with an oral medication such as ivermectin will prevent infection. At least one preventive (selamectin) is available as a topical "spot-on"—a liquid that you apply to a small area of skin. An injectable heartworm preventive that lasts for six months can be used in dogs that are more than six months old. Puppies can be started on some heartworm preventives as early as four weeks of age, but must be tested for heartworms six months to one year later. If your Mini is older than six months, he should be tested for heartworms before you start him on preventive. After that, he'll need to be retested every one to three years to make sure he didn't become infected prior to starting the preventive or while he was taking it (this is especially important if he didn't get all his doses). Retesting is important because some heartworm preventives can cause allergic-type reactions in dogs with preexisting heartworm infection. Symptoms usually involve digestive tract upset, especially diarrhea, but in rare cases shock and death can occur.

TIP

Preventive Power

Some heartworm preventive medications also control roundworms, hookworms, and whipworms.

If you live in a warm climate, you'll need to give your Mini heartworm preventive year-round. If your climate is seasonal, you may be able to stop giving the preventive during the winter months. Check with your veterinarian to find out which preventive your Mini needs, how long you should give it, and when to test for heartworms.

External Parasites

Fleas

Fleas are the most common parasite of the dog. Although fleas have no wings, they are able to jump great distances and use this ability to move easily from dog to dog or from the environment onto a dog. Adult fleas (the only ones that bite) spend most of their time on the animal. They lay their eggs there, but the eggs quickly fall off onto the animal's bed (or your bed), carpet, or furniture. After the eggs hatch, the immature fleas feed on organic debris and flea excrement. When they mature into adults, they hop back on the animal to feed on blood and eventually reproduce. Fleas torment dogs in a number of ways. Their feeding and movement can cause localized itching and inflammation. Some dogs are allergic to flea saliva and develop generalized dermatitis. Severely infested dogs, especially

---

TIP

Call for Backup

If you still have a flea problem after you've treated your Mini, your house, and your yard, consult a professional exterminator.

---

puppies or older dogs with concurrent disease, may become anemic due to chronic blood loss.

Fleas like to run and hide, so it may be difficult to see them on your Mini. You may be able to spot them on his neck, abdomen, and the base of his tail—favorite flea hang-outs. Even if you don't see the actual critters, you'll probably find flea excrement—dark, reddish brown material that looks like specks of dirt.

Controlling fleas can be difficult, since they can survive for long periods of time in the environment, especially under warm, humid conditions. Effective treatment consists of eliminating the fleas on your Mini and eliminating them from areas where he's been. The most effective flea control products disrupt the flea life cycle by killing the adult fleas and/or the eggs. These products are available in a variety of forms—collars, oral medications, sprays, and spot-ons.

Thoroughly vacuuming your home will eliminate some of the flea eggs and larvae. It also removes flea excrement and stimulates young adult fleas to leave their protective cocoons, which makes them more vulnerable to pesticides. Put moth balls/crystals, flea powder, or a few pieces of a flea collar in the vacuum bag or canister to kill the vacuumed-up pests. After vacuuming, remove the bag, seal it in a plastic bag, and throw it away in an outside trash container.

To control fleas in your yard, treat it with a spray that combines an insecticide and insect growth regulator. You don't have to treat the entire yard, just your Mini's favorite spots (especially if they're shady) and frequently-traveled paths.

Ticks

Ticks don't just bite, they can cause anemia (especially in puppies) and transmit serious

= TIP =

Help Wanted

If your Mini has a tick that's embedded in a sensitive or hard-to-reach area, such as near an eye or in an ear, you may need to have your veterinarian remove it.

diseases, such as Rocky Mountain spotted fever and Lyme disease, to dogs and people.

Female ticks feed on the dog, breed, then drop off to lay their eggs and die. After hatching, the larval ticks ("seed ticks") attach themselves to grass and foliage to wait for a passing host. The larvae go through several stages of engorgement and molting to become adults, after which the cycle is repeated.

To remove a tick from your Mini, grasp the pest with your fingers or tweezers as close to the skin as possible and slowly pull it off. If part of the head stays behind, don't worry; this usually just causes a localized infection that will clear up on its own. After you've removed the tick, wash the area (and your hands) with mild antiseptic soap.

Some ticks can cause paralysis in dogs by injecting salivary toxins when they feed. A single tick, especially if it's embedded on or near the head, can cause the paralysis. At first the affected dog may be uncoordinated in the rear quarters, but complete paralysis develops rapidly and spreads forward. Paralysis of the respiratory muscles can result in death. Removal of the offending tick(s) usually results in rapid recovery. Tick paralysis can be prevented by prompt removal of ticks, since it takes at least

four days of feeding for signs of paralysis to develop.

Ticks can be very difficult to control, but newer products on the market make it easier—and safer—than in the past. Some spot-on products repel and kill ticks (and control fleas and sometimes mosquitoes) for 30 days with just one application. Some tick collars provide protection for three months. Regardless of which product you choose for your Mini, it's still a good idea to check your Mini for ticks every day.

Complete tick control, like flea control, involves treating your yard as well as your Mini.
✔ Eliminate tick hiding places by keeping your lawn mowed and free from overgrown brush.
✔ Fence your yard to keep tick-bearing wildlife such as deer out of it.

✔ Spray your yard with a product specifically formulated for tick control, which will keep the pests at bay for about a month. Many of these products also control fleas.

Mites

Demodex canis is a tiny elongated parasite that lives in the hair follicles and sebaceous glands of the skin. This normal skin inhabitant doesn't usually cause problems if the dog's immune system is functioning normally. Puppies sometimes develop localized demodicosis—small, red, hairless patches that usually go away without treatment. If the Demodex mites multiply unchecked, however, the result is generalized demodicosis (demodectic mange), with widespread itching, hair loss, and skin inflammation. Secondary bacterial and fungal infections worsen the skin problems and make treatment more difficult.

Veterinarians diagnose demodectic mange with a test called a skin scraping—a microscopic examination of cells and debris scraped from the skin.

If your Mini develops demodectic mange, don't try to treat it on your own. The condition that allowed the mites to multiply, the mite infestation itself, and any secondary infections must all be treated. Your veterinarian may prescribe oral anti-mite medication and medicated dips for the primary disease; oral antibiotics and antifungal medications are used to treat secondary infections. Treatment may take four months or longer. Some cases, especially those in older dogs, cannot be cured, only controlled.

Dogs are also susceptible to infestation with *Sarcoptes scabiei*, mites that cause sarcoptic mange or scabies. These parasites burrow into the skin and cause intense irritation and itching. Dried blood and serum encrust the inflamed skin, which eventually becomes wrinkled and thickened. Hair loss is widespread. Treatment for sarcoptic mange is similar to that for generalized demodicosis. People can contract sarcoptic mange from dogs, but this is relatively rare.

Ear Mites

Ear mites live in the external ear canal where they cause inflammation and severe itching. A dog with ear mites may abrade the skin of the head and ears by scratching and head rubbing. Violent head-shaking may cause an aural hematoma, an injury in which blood accumulates between the cartilage and skin of the ear flap. Ear mites typically cause the ear wax to become dark brown, so that the ear appears to have dirt or dried blood inside it. The infection is diagnosed by observing the pests during an otoscopic examination. (The warmth from the otoscope's light makes the mites move around, which makes them easy to see.) If your Mini has ear mites, your veterinarian can prescribe appropriate medication. In addition to treating your Mini, you'll need to treat all your dogs and cats because ear mites move readily from animal to animal.

Dental Care

Proper care of the teeth is important for the overall health of your Miniature Schnauzer. Dogs don't usually get cavities, but they're quite susceptible to periodontal disease—gingivitis, periodontitis, and periodontal abscesses. Gingivitis (inflammation of the gums) is most commonly caused by plaque, a soft, colorless scum that coats the teeth, especially those of dogs fed soft diets. Calculus (tartar), the hard yellowish or brown deposits found on the teeth of many dogs, promotes the formation of plaque.

Chronic gingivitis can lead to periodontitis and periodontal abscesses, which can destroy the supporting structures that hold the teeth in place. When this happens, the tooth is lost.

You can help keep your Mini's teeth plaque-free by brushing them each day with a soft-bristled toothbrush and toothpaste formulated for dogs. Feeding him dry dog food (or a tartar-control food) and giving him resilient chew toys may also decrease plaque and tartar accumulation. At least once a year, your veterinarian should examine your Mini's mouth, taking radiographs (X-rays), if necessary, and clean his

Tooth Trouble

With proper care, your Mini's teeth will last a lifetime. Check with your veterinarian if you notice any of the following signs of trouble:
- Difficulty eating
- Bad breath
- Yellow or brown teeth
- Loose, broken, or missing teeth
- Mouth injuries
- Inflamed or bleeding gums
- Pus between gums and teeth
- Retained deciduous (puppy) teeth

teeth, preferably under general anesthesia. Your veterinarian may also apply fluoride or sealants to the teeth to strengthen them and inhibit plaque formation.

Saying Good-bye

It's always difficult to say good-bye to the beloved companion with whom you've shared so much. It's even harder when you're the one who must make the decision to end your dog's life. Nevertheless, there are certain situations in which euthanasia must be considered. Even with the best of veterinary care, some diseases are still incurable and some injuries will not heal. Sometimes dogs with certain conditions can live relatively normal lives for variable periods of time. In other cases, prolonging life means prolonging pain and suffering.

There's no simple way to make the decision about euthanasia. If you are faced with this responsibility, consider your Mini first. Your feelings are important, of course, but you should not decide against euthanasia simply because of the grief you will experience. Keep in mind how sad you would be seeing your friend suffer and slowly die from an incurable illness or injury.

Euthanasia is performed by giving the dog an injection of a drug that is similar to an anesthetic, only much stronger. As the injection is made, the dog loses consciousness and then dies quickly and painlessly. Some owners prefer to remain with their dogs during euthanasia, but it can be very upsetting. For this reason, many owners choose to say their good-byes and then leave the room. The choice is yours; do whatever you feel is most comforting for you and your special friend.

If your Miniature Schnauzer gets sick or injured, you might need to give your friend a little nursing care.

Restraint

You may need to restrain your Mini before you can administer medications or treatments. Some dogs need only verbal reassurance, but others may require fairly extreme measures, such as being muzzled or restrained by a strong assistant.

Let your buddy's personality and reaction determine the restraint; always use the least amount needed to complete the task. Reassure him continually whenever any type of restraint is used.

You'll be able to perform your job more quickly if you have a helper hold your Mini. The assistant should tuck the dog under one arm, placing the hand on the chest or grasping the front legs, if necessary. The other hand, which is brought under the head to cup the cheek and skull area (on the side away from the assistant's body), holds the dog's head close to the assistant's body. Even a gentle dog may bite when stressed or in pain, so your helper should always keep your Mini at

waist level to avoid being bitten in the face. If you need to muzzle your Mini, you can use a purchased muzzle or you can make one. To make a muzzle, take a 30-inch (75 cm) length of 2-inch (5 cm) gauze (or any soft, strong material) and tie a loose overhand knot in the center of it to form a loop.

Holding the ends of the gauze, guide the loop (with the knot on top) over your dog's nose and pull the loop *tight*. Next, bring the gauze ends under the lower jaw and tie another half-hitch. Finally, bring the ends behind your Miniature Schnauzer's head and tie them in a bow (it's easy to untie). Make sure all of your ties are very tight. If they aren't, the muzzle won't work.

Taking Your Miniature Schnauzer's Temperature

To take your Mini's temperature, place a dab of lubricant (K-Y Jelly or petroleum jelly) on the end of the thermometer, turn it on if it's electronic, and gently insert it about one inch (2.5 cm) into the rectum. Hold the thermometer in place (it's easier if you hold your Mini's tail and the thermometer together) for two to three

minutes or, for an electronic thermometer, until it beeps to signal that it's finished.

Giving Medication

Oral Medication

A simple way to give your Miniature Schnauzer a pill is to place the pill in a small ball of canned dog food or a piece of soft cheese and offer it as a "treat." This will probably work well if your Mini's appetite is normal. If he won't eat the dog food or cheese ball, however, you'll have to give the pill by placing it in his mouth.

Sit to the side of your pal with one forearm (your left, if you're right-handed) on his back and the hand coming up over his head (between his eyes) to grasp his muzzle with the thumb on one side and the fingers on the other. With the other hand (holding the pill) on the lower jaw, gently tilt your Mini's head up. His mouth will probably open slightly. Open his mouth more widely and quickly place the pill as far back as possible on the middle of the tongue. Close his mouth, hold it shut, and rub his throat. Be sure to tell him what a good dog he is. After about a minute, let him open his mouth. If he spits the pill out, try again.

To give your Mini liquid medication, put the liquid in an oral dose syringe or large plastic eyedropper. Gently tilt your pal's head up and insert the syringe or dropper in the corner of his mouth between the cheek and teeth. Slowly dribble the liquid into his mouth. Most dogs will simply swallow the liquid.

Eye Medication

When applying eye medication, which usually comes in ointment or drop form, it's important to avoid touching the eye with the applicator or your fingers. Most dogs tolerate application of eye ointment better than eye drops.

To apply ointment, gently pull your Mini's lower eyelid down and deposit a ribbon of oint-ment inside it. Close the eyelids with your fin-gers to distribute the ointment.

To apply eye drops, tilt your buddy's head up, gently hold the eyelids apart, and quickly deposit the drops in the inside corner of the eye or inside the lower eyelid. Hold the dropper close to the eye—you're less likely to miss your target and it's more comfortable for your pal.

Ear Medication

To apply ear medication, raise your Mini's earflap (if his ears are uncropped), tilt his head so the affected ear is up, and place the medication in the ear canal. Hold your buddy's head so he doesn't shake the medication out. Gently mas-sage the ear to help distribute the medication.

Topical Medication

Topical medication—usually an ointment but sometimes a liquid—is applied to the skin.

Your Miniature Schnauzer will be more likely to swallow a pill placed on the middle of the tongue as far back in the mouth as possible.

Ointment can be applied directly to the skin or you can apply it with your finger. Drops are usually applied directly to the skin. After apply-ing either type of medication, rub it in well (unless otherwise instructed by your veterinar-ian). The greatest difficulty with topical med-ication is keeping the patient from licking it off before it has a chance to work. Taking your Mini for a walk or playing with him may dis-tract him enough so that he loses interest in trying to remove the medication.

GROOMING YOUR MINIATURE SCHNAUZER

No doubt about it: keeping your Miniature Schnauzer well groomed will take some effort. You'll probably want to leave clipping and trimming to a professional groomer, but the day-to-day brushing, combing, and general fussing can be fun for both you and your Mini.

The Right Start to Good Grooming

Many dog owners simply assume that their dog will enjoy being bathed and groomed. So, without any advance warning, they unceremoniously plunk their canine companion into the bathtub, or start tugging at her coat with brushes and combs. When grooming activities are presented in this fashion, it's no wonder that the dog is often less than enthusiastic about it all.

When your Miniature Schnauzer is just a puppy, accustom her gradually to grooming routines. Make grooming a fun and enjoyable ritual. Brush her frequently, but for very short periods, using a soft brush. Lavishly praise her when she sits still. Wipe her eyes, swab the leathers of her ears, handle her paws. If she

gets nervous about any particular activity, stop and reassure her, then briefly go back to what you were doing. (You don't want her to think that all she has to do is whine and you'll give it up completely.) Praise her when she allows you to continue. Keep working with your Mini puppy until she quietly lets you perform all the necessary grooming chores except bathing. (You don't need to worry about bathing her until she's at least six months old.)

At-Home Care or Professional Grooming?

Proper grooming of the Miniature Schnauzer involves trimming with scissors and electric clippers. Many owners prefer not to undertake the trimming chores themselves. Instead, they opt to have their dogs professionally clipped by a pro-

fessional groomer. Most groomers include bathing, nail-trimming, and ear-cleaning as part of the clipping appointment, but it's still the owner's responsibility to properly groom the dog between visits. Because so many Miniature Schnauzer owners choose to have their dogs professionally clipped, this chapter outlines grooming tasks that owners are more likely to perform at home.

Bathing

Your Mini will probably need to be bathed only every six to eight weeks, usually during her regular visits to the groomer. This assumes that she doesn't come into contact with something

that dictates more immediate attention, such as tar, paint, mud, or—every owner's nightmare—a skunk! If you suddenly find yourself with a tarry, painted, muddy, or odiferous Miniature Schnauzer, you'll need to know how to give her a bath.

You'll need the following equipment:
✔ Stiff bristle or slicker brush
✔ Dog shampoo
✔ Sponge
✔ Cotton balls
✔ Bland eye ointment
✔ Several towels

On warm days, you can bathe your Mini outside, but you may find it easier to give the bath inside in a bathtub equipped with a nonskid surface or rubber mat. (Be prepared for your bathroom to get wet!)

Before giving the bath, brush your pal's coat with the bristle or slicker brush. Carefully remove any plant material, such as burrs or sticks, from the coat before bathing (don't forget to check her ears and between her toes). If your Mini has gotten into tar or paint, you may need to cut out the affected hair. Never use turpentine, kerosene, or gasoline to remove tar or paint from the coat. If you don't want to cut the coat, soak the affected areas in vegetable or mineral oil for 24 hours and then shampoo.

Place a small cotton ball in your Mini's ears to keep water and shampoo out of them during the bath. Apply a small amount of bland eye ointment to her eyes to protect them.

Adjust the flow and temperature of the water before you put your Mini in the tub. The water temperature should be comfortably warm, not hot. Continually check during the bath to make sure it doesn't get too hot or too cold.

Place your Mini in the tub. After she's settled a bit, thoroughly wet her coat. Apply a small amount of shampoo with the sponge—you can always add more if you need to—and work up a lather. Massage the lather into your pal's coat. Rinse thoroughly; a spray hose helps, but you can also use a pan or other container. Repeat the shampooing and rinsing. Squeeze the excess water out of the coat.

Now comes the tricky part—getting that wet dog out of the tub and into a towel before she shakes water all over you and the bathroom. If you're quick, you can pounce on her with a large, thirsty towel and hold her in your arms until you can dry her off a bit (it's nice that Miniature Schnauzers are small). Or you can pull the shower curtain around the tub and let her shake away.

After towel drying your buddy, you can complete the drying process with a hair dryer (set no higher than warm) or, if it's a warm day, simply let her air dry. This latter option sounds good for a hot summer day, but only if you have a clean area, like a patio, where you can confine her. Otherwise, she might just run out and undo all your good work. Also remember that air-conditioning can make her cold even on a hot day.

For those times when a bath with conventional shampoo and water isn't possible, dry shampoo will clean your Mini without using water. These products are also convenient for spot cleaning.

Skunked!

If your Mini has had a close encounter with a skunk, determine which body parts got blasted (usually the face and front end) and trim away any long hair in the area, if possible. Next, bathe your buddy with regular dog shampoo. If you can, give the bath before the skunk spray has dried.

Your next step: getting rid of the rest of the stink. Pet supply stores carry several types of deskunking products—solutions, powders, and shampoos. If you don't have any of these products on hand, you can try massaging tomato juice or double-strength instant coffee (warm, not hot) into your Mini's coat. Rinse with water and repeat, if necessary. You can also make your own deskunking compound by combining one quart of hydrogen peroxide (3 percent) with ¼ cup baking soda and one teaspoonful of liquid dishwashing soap in an open container (the mixture will fizz). Mix the ingredients immediately before use. Bathe your pal in the mixture, avoiding the eyes and mouth (use a cloth to apply it to the face). Discard any unused mixture.

Skunk spray can irritate your Mini's eyes and throat, causing redness, swelling, and pain, especially if she takes a "direct hit" or the incident occurs in close quarters such as a burrow. Consult your veterinarian if your pal shows any signs of these, especially if she's having trouble breathing.

Skunks can carry rabies so make sure your Mini's rabies vaccination is always current.

Coat Care

Regular brushing between grooming appointments will help keep your Miniature Schnauzer's coat and skin healthy. First brush her gently with a slicker brush or stiff bristle brush, then follow with a metal comb to remove any dead hairs. If she has matted hair that you can't tease apart with the comb, carefully cut longitudinally

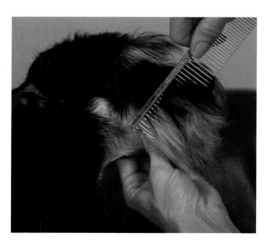

through the mat (in several places if necessary), then comb to remove the mat. Always cut away from the body and remember to work slowly and gently; removing mats almost always tugs on the skin. If your Mini has a lot of mats, you might want to have your groomer remove them. This may require substantial clipping.

Ear Care

Under normal circumstances, your Mini's ears don't need elaborate care, other than an occasional cleaning and periodic checking for foreign bodies (such as burrs or grass awns) or signs of infections or ear mites.

To clean your pal's ears, you'll need cotton balls, cotton swabs, and canine ear-cleaning solution (from your veterinarian or at the pet supply store). Never use irritating substances such as alcohol on or in the ears. Apply a few drops of the ear-cleaning solution to the underside of the ear flap, then place the tip of the bottle in the ear canal's opening (don't force the tip into the ear canal) and squeeze a small amount of solution into the ear. After letting your Mini shake her head to get rid of the excess solution, massage the base of the ear for 20 to 30 seconds. Use a cotton ball or swab to clean the underside of the ear flap. Remove dirt and debris from the ear canal with a cotton ball, not a swab, so you don't push ear gunk further into the canal.

Take your Mini to the veterinarian if you notice signs of an ear problem: abnormal odor, discharge, head-shaking, excessive scratching, or pain. If she has a foreign body in her ear, remove it, if possible, but only if you can easily see and grasp it. Otherwise, let your veterinarian take care of the problem.

Nail Trimming

Many dogs need to have their nails trimmed every four to six weeks. Dogs that spend a lot of time inside need more frequent attention; outside dogs that regularly exercise on hard surfaces require less. Your groomer will probably trim your Mini's nails, but you should check weekly to make sure they're not getting too long.

It usually helps to have someone assist you with nail trimming, especially if you and your Miniature Schnauzer are both new to it. Have your assistant hold your Mini and talk to her to distract her a bit. Grasp the paw and gently spread the toes. If your Mini's toenails are black, just nip the sharp point off the end of each one. If the nails are white, you'll be able to see a pinkish core—the quick—in the center of the nail. Try not to cut into the quick; it hurts and the nail will bleed. Continue trimming until you've done all of the nails. Don't forget the dewclaws if your Mini has them.

If you accidentally clip a nail too short (it happens—even to veterinarians and groomers), your canine companion will probably protest loudly and dramatically. It hurts, of course, but the pain will soon subside. The nail will bleed, which may be a bit alarming; bleeding from a nail can be more difficult to stop than bleeding from a similarly sized wound somewhere else on the body. That's partly because there's no soft tissue around the blood vessel (since it's in the middle of the nail), but mostly because a dog that's been "quicked" usually bounces around a lot, which increases the bleeding. Don't worry—dogs don't bleed to death from injured toenails. You can apply a styptic pencil or anticoagulant stick to the end of the nail or dip the nail in a bit of flour. If, for some reason, you don't have access to either of these remedies, you can

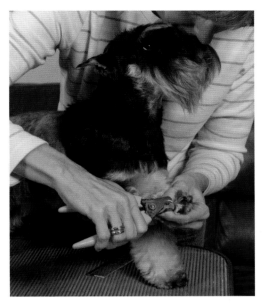

apply gentle pressure to the end of the nail with a small piece of tissue or cotton for about five minutes. Most importantly, be sure to give your "injured" friend lots of sympathy!

Anal Sacs

The anal sacs (also called anal glands) are two small pouchlike structures located on either side of the rectum. These sacs produce a very odiferous substance that is normally expressed when the dog has a bowel movement. If your Mini's anal sacs don't empty, it will make her uncomfortable. She may scoot her rear end on the ground or chew at her anal area in an effort to relieve her discomfort. Some manuals advise owners to check their dog's anal sacs and express them if there seems to be a problem, but most owners prefer to let their veterinarian handle this rather unpleasant task.

TRAINING YOUR MINIATURE SCHNAUZER

Miniature Schnauzers learn quickly, so it won't be hard to teach your pal manners and basic obedience commands. You'll both have fun and the training process will strengthen the bond between you and your Mini.

Why Train My Mini?

When you train your Mini, you'll teach him simple good manners such as walking on a leash without pulling or not begging at the table, as well as basic obedience commands (*sit*, *lie down*, *heel*, *stay*, and *come*). As a result, he'll be a more pleasant companion. Training will also give your Mini a job (with you, his favorite person!), warding off boredom, which often leads to destructive habits. Training can even protect your pal because you'll have better control of him. For example, if he slipped out of the house, your command to *"come"* would bring him back before he reached the street. Finally, training lets your Mini know that

you're the "pack leader," which makes it easier for you to control him under all circumstances.

Learn to Train

There are several ways that you can learn to train your Miniature Schnauzer:

✔ Attend obedience classes. In an obedience class, you'll learn to train your Mini; your Mini will learn basic obedience commands and gain socialization skills from working around other dogs and their owners.

✔ Work individually with a trainer. This option appeals to owners who prefer one-on-one instruction. Private sessions with a trainer are more expensive than classes, but you and your Mini will get more individual attention.

✔ Send your Mini to obedience school. With this option, a professional trainer teaches the dog basic obedience commands. Since the trainer works directly with the dog, it's a very effective method of training. The best programs include some sessions with the owner handling the dog.

✔ Do-it-yourself. This method may work for you, especially if you're an experienced dog owner. If not, you may run into problems that are hard to solve. It helps to have a trainer that you can consult.

When and Where

You can start training your Mini puppy when he's as young as nine weeks of age, as long as the lessons are short and simple; his ability to

concentrate will be limited. If you want to enroll your youngster in a "puppy kindergarten" class, get your veterinarian's approval first; his puppy vaccinations may not completely protect him from contagious diseases. Your veterinarian may recommend that you wait until he's at least four months of age before exposing him to large numbers of dogs.

On the other end of the age span, there's no limit for training, even if your Mini is a senior. You may have to make a few concessions for an older dog (for instance, he might not be as agile as he once was), but beyond that, you definitely *can* teach an old dog new tricks.

Formal training sessions should take place in an area where you and your Mini have some room to move around. When you're just starting out, choose a spot that's free from major distractions such as loose dogs and shouting children. Limit your training periods to one or two per day. Keep each session short, starting with about 5 minutes and gradually working up to 15 to 30 minutes per session. After each lesson, take a few minutes to play with your student.

If this type of schedule won't work for you, don't give up. Any time spent training your Mini will yield positive results. You may be able to work with him only for 15 or 20 minutes several times a week. That's okay. It will take longer to reach your training goals, but any time spent training your pal will eventually pay off. Many dogs have learned basic manners and obedience commands during repeated lessons that never lasted more than five minutes.

Consider your dog's mental attitude before you start a training session. For instance, don't expect him to concentrate on training when you've just come home from being gone all day. Some particularly bouncy dogs benefit from a brisk walk or run before lessons. Just be sure to allow some calm-down time before class.

Not all of your Miniature Schnauzer's training will take place during regularly scheduled sessions; some of it will occur as you teach and reinforce appropriate behavior during the course of your daily routine. In addition, doing a little "homework"—giving your Mini specific commands whenever possible throughout the day (for example, making him sit for a treat)—will greatly increase the effectiveness of his structured obedience lessons.

Equipment

You don't need a lot of equipment to train your Mini, but you do need the right kind of equipment. First, you'll need a training collar—a collar that tightens when pressure is applied on the leash, then loosens immediately when the pressure is released. There are three types of training collars: slip-on, snap-around, and pinch.

✔ **Slip-on collars**, which are made of chain or nylon, are inexpensive and easy to put on. They don't fit as closely as snap-on collars, so the dog doesn't pick up the handler's signals as quickly.

✔ **Snap-around collars**, which are made of nylon, are harder to put on, but fit closely and provide precise control. They're more expensive than slip-on collars, but still reasonably priced.

✔ **Pinch collars** are made of chain, with blunt prongs that tighten around the dog's neck when pressure is applied. They're wicked-looking, but actually quite safe—unlike the other collars, a pinch collar cannot cut off the dog's air. These collars, available in sizes ranging from extra-small (micro) to large, are very effective, especially for dogs that pull a lot or otherwise ignore their handlers during training sessions.

The second item of equipment that you'll need is a leash. It should be made of canvas, nylon, or leather, ½ to 1 inch (1.3–2.5 cm) wide and 6 feet (1.8 m) long.

Many owners balk at the idea of using a training collar (especially a pinch collar) on their dog, arguing that training collars are cruel, dangerous devices and a regular collar is just as effective. A properly used training collar is neither cruel nor dangerous. Constant tension is never applied. Rather, the trainer quickly applies just the amount of correction needed at the precise moment it is needed. When the correction is finished (a matter of seconds), the collar loosens to its original position. Use of a regular collar would cause more discomfort, because the corrections would be less effective and necessitate more constant pressure on the collar.

Before you start your training sessions, give your Mini a chance to become familiar with the training collar and leash. Let him wear the collar while in the house under your direct supervision. Once he's used to the collar, snap the leash on and let him drag it around inside, always keeping him where you can watch him. Praise him when he accepts his training gear.

Correction and Praise

Every dog needs discipline and correction during training sessions. The amount of correction required depends on your dog's personality (stubborn vs. tractable). It also depends on whether you have allowed your canine buddy to get away with certain unacceptable behaviors. If this is the case, your corrections may have to be quite strong, especially at first, to demonstrate that you're serious about your request.

Your most effective tools of discipline will be your voice and the training collar. Reprimands—a simple "No!" should suffice—should be spoken firmly and confidently without yelling. Corrections with the collar consist of a *check*—a quick snap on the leash, followed by an immediate release. It's better to repeat the check than to maintain constant tension on the leash.

After you correct your Mini, praise him as soon as possible. Find some little thing and offer a word of praise and a pat on the head. This reassures your friend that no permanent rift in your relationship has occurred.

During the training session, your pupil will be on your left side. Hold the leash in your left hand, with the excess loosely coiled in your right hand. Give commands in a clear, firm voice, always preceding them with your dog's name ("*Happy, sit!*"). Correction consists of a check with only as much force as needed. Try to be consistent; let your pal know that you expect him to obey immediately and that correction will always occur if he doesn't. Remember to praise your Mini when he does what you want him to do and also after every correction.

In addition to teaching basic manners and obedience commands, you should also teach your buddy a release command, a simple word such as *"Okay"* to let him know he can relax and move around. For example, if you've put your Mini in a *sit*, the release command tells him he doesn't have to sit anymore.

Basic Mini Manners

In order to be a well-mannered companion, your Miniature Schnauzer should know the following commands: *sit, down, come, easy, go lie down*, and *leave it*.

Sit

For the *sit*, your Mini will sit at your left side, facing straight ahead with head and shoulders square to your knee. While your Mini stands beside you, give the command, *"Happy, sit!"* Let go of the leash with your left hand and use this hand to guide your dog's hindquarters into a sitting position. At the same time, hold his head up with the leash in your right hand. (Remember to praise!) Have your pupil stay sitting for a few seconds, then give the release command. After a few minutes repeat the sitting exercise.

Gradually increase the time that your buddy stays in the sitting position.

Down

In obedience training, the command *"Down!"* means lie down, not get down. To teach this command, have your Mini sit by your side. Kneel down and reach over his back with your left arm and grasp his left front leg near the body. At the same time, grasp his right front leg near his body with your right hand. Give the command, *"Happy, down!"* and gently position him by lifting the forequarters off the ground and easing his body down. This maneuver is designed to prevent any struggles between you and your pupil. He won't mind having your arms around him—you're his best friend, after all—and he won't be able to resist the command by bracing his front legs. Once your pal is down, slowly release your hold on his legs and let your left hand rest on his back, while repeating the *down* command. After a few seconds, give him the release command, and have him sit so you can try it again. Keep working until you no longer have to position him; then work until he'll lie down while you remain standing.

Come

Anyone who's ever tried to catch a runaway dog can tell you that *"Come!"* is one of the most important commands a dog can learn. To teach your Mini to come on command, have him sit, then move away the distance of the leash. Kneel down and enthusiastically say, *"Happy, come!"* Hold your arms out, pat your knees, do whatever you can to coax him to you. Because you're best buddies, he'll probably come bounding up to you. When he reaches you, quickly give the command to sit. You may

have to reinforce it by guiding him into position. Have him sit for a few seconds then praise him. Continue working like this, gradually increasing the distance you move away before calling him. Use a longer leash to practice greater distances, if necessary.

Easy

A well-mannered dog walks quietly on a leash without pulling. This doesn't mean your Mini needs to heel, although that's a useful command too, only that he shouldn't tug on the leash. To teach the *easy* command, hold the end of the leash in both hands (don't put the loop over your wrist) and anchor them firmly at the level of your waist. Give your Mini the command, *"Happy, let's go!"* and start walking. When Happy bounds ahead, as he almost certainly will, say *"Happy, easy!"* then turn to the right and walk in the opposite direction. If possible, try to make your turn before he gets to the end of the leash. When he catches up to

30 minutes. Always remember to give him the release command when it's okay for him to leave his spot.

Leave It

With your Mini on a leash, walk by a tempting item such as a treat or a toy (pre-place the items, if you wish). When your pal tries to pick up the item, give a quick check on the leash and say, "*Happy, leave it!*" Praise him when he obeys. You can reward him with a treat, but cheerful words and ear scratches work well too. Repeat the lesson at home and other locations.

Another method of teaching this command involves holding a treat in your closed fist. When your Mini noses your hand, say, "*Happy, leave it!*" and keep your fist closed. When he stops nosing your hand, praise him, then give the release command ("*Okay!*") and let him have the treat. Continue the lessons until he'll sit quietly without touching a nearby treat until you give the release command.

Other Obedience Commands

Heel

To teach your Miniature Schnauzer to heel, position him at your left side and start to walk, giving the command, "*Happy, heel!*" At the same time, lightly snap the leash to encourage him to walk beside you. Continue to encourage him with light snaps, if necessary, praising after every snap. Your pupil's neck and shoulder should be even with your left leg. If your Mini charges ahead, give the leash a light check and repeat the command to heel. Repeat the check as needed, but never put continuous pressure on the leash. Practice heeling in short, brief

you, praise him. Repeat the lesson until he'll walk on a slack leash.

Go Lie Down

This command tells your pal to go to a designated spot and lie down. First, choose the spot—it can be his crate, bed, or even just a special rug. Next, take your Mini to the spot and tell him "*Happy, go lie down!*" If you've already taught him the *down* command, he'll probably lie down. When he does, praise him. After five seconds, give him the release command. Gradually increase the distance he has to go to get to his spot. If he doesn't understand what he's supposed to do, gently take him there and praise him when he lies down. Also increase the time he remains in the spot, until he'll stay there for sessions. Once your pal has mastered heeling while walking in a straight line, add corners, circles, and maneuvers around obstacles.

When heeling, your Mini should sit whenever you stop moving (unless you give another command). To teach this, have him heel for 15 to 20 seconds, then stop walking and simultaneously tell him to sit. After he sits for a few seconds, give the *heel* command and start walking. After a short distance, stop again and repeat the command to sit. Continue working like this until your pal sits automatically whenever you stop walking.

Stay

During a sitting *stay*, your Mini should remain in a sitting position until released by your command. Have him sit by your side while on the leash. Give the command, "*Happy, stay!*" and step a few feet away from him while still holding the leash. Repeat the command. He'll probably try to come with you, especially if you've taught him to heel. If he does, tell him "*No!*" and put him back into position, repeating the *stay* command. Have him stay for about ten seconds, then give the release command. Continue working on the *stay* until your Mini will remain in place for at least three minutes after just one command. You can also gradually increase the distance you move away. If you like, repeat the lessons using the *down* position instead of the *sit*.

Beyond Basic Training

Once your Mini has mastered the basic obedience lessons on the leash, you might want to try some off-leash work. Before you unsnap that leash, however, make sure your pal obeys

all of your commands without hesitation. To work off-leash, have your Mini sit by your side, then simply take the leash off and proceed with a regular training session. If he has lapses in obedience, put the leash back on him and correct as necessary. Concentrate your training on the problem areas, then remove the leash for another try.

After your Mini has completed "basic training," you might want to work on advanced obedience training, which involves more complicated exercises such as retrieving objects, jumping hurdles, and extended *stays*.

You can watch dogs performing at this level in obedience classes at many AKC dog shows. If you'd like to do more advanced work with your Miniature Schnauzer, consult your local kennel club or professional dog trainer about advanced obedience classes.

HAVING FUN WITH YOUR MINIATURE SCHNAUZER

Just living with a Miniature Schnauzer is fun, but there are all kinds of special activities that the two of you can enjoy together.

Trick and Treat

All dogs should know basic obedience commands, but this doesn't mean that everything you teach your Mini has to be serious or even particularly useful for anything beyond sheer entertainment. A repertoire of clever tricks can be fun for you to teach and fun for your canine friend to learn.

You can teach your friend all sorts of tricks. Shaking hands is a standard, but dogs can also be taught to play dead, hold the end of their own leash (or even another dog's leash—with the dog attached), balance things on the end of their nose, roll over, and many others. You can also teach your Mini to "speak" or "sing," but you might regret it if it leads to unwanted barking. You can find books about training dogs to do tricks at local or Internet bookstores or the public library. You can also check some of the many dog-related Web sites on the Internet for information about it. If you have a friend whose dog performs tricks, you might ask for help with your trick-training efforts.

Walking and Jogging

Your Mini will undoubtedly enjoy going with you when you walk or jog. Before you head for the trail, take time to consider your friend's comfort and safety.

✔ Get your veterinarian's okay ahead of time, especially if your Mini is a "senior citizen" or has ongoing health problems.

✔ Keep your pal on a leash at all times.

✔ Make sure your Mini carries proper identification—a collar tag, tattoo, or microchip.

✔ Avoid areas with loose dogs. Even if they're friendly, they can be distracting and annoying. If they're not friendly, they can spell disaster for you and your Mini.

✔ Watch the weather. Don't exercise strenuously when it's extremely hot, particularly if it's also humid. Rain won't hurt either of you, but be sure to dry your Mini off when you get home. Cold weather won't cause many problems, unless it's bitterly cold (in which case, you'll probably stay home anyway), because the exercise will help you both stay warm. If you walk or jog on snow, check your Mini's feet frequently and remove any snow that may be balled up between her toes. If the sidewalks and streets have been treated with chemicals to melt the snow, be sure to wash off her feet when you get home.

In some towns, dog owners gather informally once or twice a week to walk or jog with their dogs. This is a good way to meet other dog lovers and it can help your Mini get used to being around other dogs. Ask your dog-owning friends about groups in your town or area. If there aren't any, you might want to organize one yourself.

Organized Activities

Even if you enjoy mainly informal activities with your Miniature Schnauzer, you may want to investigate some of the organized activities that are available in your community. These activities may be relatively simple (membership in a local dog club) or more complicated and time-consuming (showing in recognized dog shows or obedience trials).

Dog Clubs

Dog clubs, which may be all-breed or breed-specific, can be found in many larger towns and cities. In more sparsely populated areas, dog clubs may be comprised of members from a wide region of the state. In addition to regular meetings, dog clubs organize activities such as puppy matches, informal dog shows that help inexperienced dogs or owners prepare for the stiffer competition of AKC-recognized shows. For information about dog clubs in your area, check the AKC Web site (*www.akc.org*) or contact AKC customer care at (919) 233-9767. A local breeder, pet supply store, or veterinarian may also be able to help you find a club near you.

AKC–Recognized Events

An intact (not spayed or neutered) Miniature Schnauzer registered by the American Kennel Club can compete in all AKC-recognized events, including conformation dog shows, obedience trials, and agility trials. Spayed or neutered Minis can't compete in conformation dog shows (which are judged on the dog's suitability for breeding) but they're eligible for all other events. Any dog, even non-purebreds, can participate in the Canine Good Citizen program.

The Canine Good Citizen (CGC) program: This program is designed to encourage owners to teach their dogs basic manners. In order to receive the Canine Good Citizen award, the dog must pass a test of the following skills:

✔ Accepting a friendly stranger.

✔ Sitting politely for petting by a stranger.

✔ Appearance and grooming (healthy, well-groomed appearance; accepting grooming and examination).

✔ Walking on a loose lead, with turns and stops.

✔ Walking through a crowd.

✔ *Sit* and *down* on command; staying in place.

✔ Coming when called.

✔ Reaction to another dog.

✔ Reaction to a distraction, such as a jogger, a chair being dropped, or a rolling crate dolly.

✔ Supervised separation (owner leaves dog and goes out of sight).

Local dog clubs or trained individuals (for example, AKC judges, 4-H leaders, or veterinarians) may administer the CGC test. You can obtain the names of clubs and CGC evaluators in your area from the AKC.

Conformation dog shows: In a conformation dog show, each dog is judged according to its official AKC breed standard (see the first chapter of this book for a summary of the Miniature Schnauzer breed standard). Dogs are initially shown against others of their breed, gender, and age. Class winners continue competing until one individual is selected as Best of Breed, which means that this dog has been judged to be the dog that most closely exemplifies the breed standard. The judge then selects the Best of Opposite Sex. All Best of Breed winners then compete against the other Best of Breed winners of their AKC Group. For example, the Best of Breed for Miniature Schnauzers would compete against all of the Best of Breed winners from the Terrier Group. Finally, the winners from each group competition compete against each other for the title of Best of Show, the highest honor awarded in a dog show. When a dog wins a certain number of points at AKC-recognized shows, it earns the title of Champion (Ch.), which is then appended to the beginning of its name (e.g., Ch. Rimview Silver Dust).

Obedience trials: In an obedience trial, it won't matter what your Mini looks like, because performance is the only thing that matters. Obedience classes are organized into Novice, Open, and Utility categories, with Novice being the easiest and Utility the most advanced. In

the Novice class, the dog performs basic exercises, including heeling (on leash and free), standing for examination, long *sit*, long *down*, and *recall*. In the Open class, the dog is required to perform more advanced exercises, such as heeling free, retrieving on the flat and over a vertical obstacle (high jump), and broad jump. In the Utility class, the dog performs the most advanced obedience tasks, such as responding to hand signals, scent discrimination, and directed retrieval exercises.

To earn an obedience title, a dog must receive qualifying scores from three different judges at three AKC-licensed or member obedience trials. To receive a qualifying score, the dog must earn more than 50 percent of the points for each exercise, with a total score of 170 points out of a possible 200. The basic obedience titles include Companion Dog (CD) at the Novice level, Companion Dog Excellent (CDX) at the Open level, and Utility Dog (UD) at the Utility level. A dog must earn the Novice

title before competing in the Open class and must earn the Open title before competing in the Utility class. Dogs that have earned the Utility Dog title are eligible to compete for the titles of Utility Dog Excellent (UDX) and Obedience Trial Champion (OTCH).

Agility trials: These are another type of AKC competition that is judged solely on performance. In these events, the dog negotiates assorted obstacles on the handler's command. Agility trials have three types of classes: Standard, Jumpers with Weaves, and FAST (Fifteen and Send Time). Standard classes contain "contact obstacles" (for example, the A-frame, dog walk, and seesaw), obstacles with a zone at each end that the dog must touch with at least one paw. Standard classes also contain jumps (adjusted for the dog's height), weave poles, tunnels, a pause table, and other obstacles. Jumpers

with Weaves classes, which have no contact obstacles or pause table, contain weave poles, jumps, and other obstacles that are negotiated as quickly as possible. The FAST class is a free-form test in which the dog negotiates 15 obstacles, in no particular order, then completes the "send bonus," two or three other obstacles in a special area where the handler is not allowed.

Agility classes are scored on both speed and accuracy. Points are deducted for going over the standard course time and for errors made on course (for example, displacing a bar on a jump or missing a contact zone).

Agility trials offer different levels of competition, including Novice (the easiest level), Open (intermediate), and Excellent (advanced). The courses become longer and more complex with each successive level. Dogs or handlers that might have difficulty in regular agility classes can compete in Preferred classes, which have lower jumps and allow more time for completion.

To receive an agility title, a dog must earn a certain number of qualifying scores in a particular class level such as Novice Standard, Open Standard, or Excellent Standard. Similar requirements apply for the Novice, Open, and Excellent Jumpers with Weaves classes. Dogs competing in Preferred division classes earn comparable titles.

Dogs that have earned their title at the Excellent level can continue to compete to earn additional qualifying scores and further titles. The highest honor an agility dog can achieve is the title of Master Agility Champion (MACH).

Rally trials: These are AKC competitions specifically designed for pet dogs and their owners. They provide a stepping stone between the Canine Good Citizen program and higher levels of competition, such as obedience or agility trials. In rally events, the dog and handler move through a course of 10 to 20 "stations," performing specific tasks at or between the stations.

The competition levels at a Rally trial include Novice, Advanced, and Excellent, with Novice being the easiest. At the Novice level, the dog performs the exercises while on the leash and the owner can use physical encouragement (for example, clapping or patting his or her leg). Examples of Novice tasks include changing pace between stations and turning 360 degrees. At the Advanced level, the dog performs off-leash, but physical encouragement is still allowed. Advanced tasks include jumping and recall to the front of the owner. At the Excellent level, the dog competes off-leash with only verbal encouragement, performing more complicated tasks, such as backing up three steps or a mov-ing stand (standing while the handler walks around the dog).

A dog that performs the required tasks according to AKC regulations receives a qualifying score (at least 70 out of a possible 100 points). The amount of time it takes the dog to complete the course doesn't affect the qualifying score, but is used to break a tie if two dogs have identical scores.

Rally titles—Rally Novice (RN), Rally Advanced (RA), and Rally Excellent (RE)—are awarded to dogs that have earned three qualifying scores from two different judges. Dogs that earn ten qualifying scores in both the advanced and excellent classes at the same trial receive the Rally Advanced Excellent (RAE) title.

Volunteer Activities

Medical experts have finally learned what dog owners have known for years: dogs are good for people! Not only that, an individual doesn't even have to own the dog to gain significant benefits.

Consequently, more and more dogs are being used to enhance the health-related therapeutic and recreational activities of hospitals, nursing homes, and rehabilitation centers. Usually these dogs are owned by people who volunteer their time and the companionship of their special canine friend.

Therapy dogs need to be well-mannered and reliable. They must be able to respond calmly to people, without jumping up, barking, or biting.

They must not be intimidated or frightened by unusual sights (such as heavily bandaged patients), sounds (such as rattling carts or beeping monitors), smells (such as disinfectant),

Your Mini, in addition to possessing many of the above characteristics, undoubtedly has other special traits. Is she especially gentle? Does she always seem to know just how you're feeling? Is she calm and well mannered even when there's a lot going on? If so, she may be perfect for volunteer work.

Several organizations help dog owners prepare their four-footed friends (and themselves) for therapy work. Some of these, such as the Delta Society (*www.deltasociety.org*), provide training workshops or home-study training courses, followed by evaluation and registration of dogs that pass the evaluation. Other organizations, such as Therapy Dogs International (*www.tdi-dog.org*), offer evaluation and registration. The specific requirements for registration vary, but in general the dog must be a minimum age (usually one year), in good health, and pass a thorough test of manners and obedience. After registration, the organizations help the owner/dog team find suitable volunteer opportunities.

If you'd like to find out more about volunteer opportunities for you and your Mini in your area, contact local hospitals, nursing homes, libraries, and schools.

If they don't have this type of program, they may be able to direct you to a facility that does. Talk to area volunteer agencies.

Veterinarians, dog breeders, or groomers might have information about dog/owner volunteer programs. It might take awhile before you find just the right opportunity, but once you do, you'll be rewarded by the knowledge that you and your Mini are vitally involved in helping others. You may find that your Miniature Schnauzer is just what the doctor ordered!

or activities (such as physical therapy treatments). They must, of course, be completely house-trained.

Miniature Schnauzers have qualities that make them well-suited for certain types of volunteer work. They're small, so they're easily transported and don't take up a lot of space, an important consideration in settings where space is limited, such as hospital rooms. Most Minis are friendly and outgoing. Some might be a little too bouncy for some situations, but certain patients, such as children, might find this particularly appealing.

Organizations

American Kennel Club
5580 Centerview Drive
Raleigh, NC 27606
(919) 233-9767
www.akc.org

American Miniature Schnauzer Club, Inc.
Amy Gordon, Secretary
342 Putnam Ranch Road
West Palm Beach, FL 33405
www.amsc.us
Note: Check the Web site for updated
information.

Canadian Kennel Club
200 Ronson Drive, Suite 400
Etobicoke, Ontario
M9W 529
(416) 675-5511
www.ckc.ca

United Kennel Club
100 E. Kilgore Road
Kalamazoo, MI 49001-5598
(269) 343-9020
www.ukcdogs.com

Books

American Kennel Club. *The Complete Dog Book.*
New York, NY: Ballantine Books, 2006.
Baer, Ted. *Communicating with Your Dog.*
Hauppauge, NY: Barron's Educational Series,
Inc., 1999.
Campbell, William E. *The New Better Behavior
in Dogs: A Guide to Solving All Your Dog
Problems.* Loveland, CO: Alpine Publications,
1999.

Eldredge, Debra M., Liisa D. Carlson, Delbert G.
Carlson, and James M. Giffin. *Dog Owner's
Home Veterinary Handbook.* Hoboken, NJ:
Howell Book House, 2007.
Frye, Frederic L. *Schnauzers.* Hauppauge, NY:
Barron's Educational Series, Inc., 2005.
Gallant, Johan. *The World of Schnauzers.*
Loveland, CO: Alpine Publications, Inc., 1996.

Magazines

AKC Gazette
AKC Family Dog
Contact AKC for subscription information.
www.akc.org

Dog Fancy
Dog World
P.O. Box 6050
Mission Viejo, CA 92690-6050
(949) 855-8822
www.dogchannel.com

About the Author

Karla S. Rugh is a 1974 graduate of the Kansas State University College of Veterinary Medicine. In addition to her D.V.M., she holds a Ph.D. in physiology and has advanced clinical training in veterinary anesthesiology. She has practiced veterinary medicine in both private and academic settings. Her academic writing has been published in prestigious journals such as the *American Journal of Physiology*, *Journal of Applied Physiology*, and *Cardiovascular Research*. Dr. Rugh is currently a freelance writer, as well as a writing consultant specializing in scientific and technical material. Having enjoyed the companionship of many dogs since early childhood, she admits that choosing her favorite breed would be a difficult task.

Acknowledgments

Unbeknownst to me, this book was begun more than 40 years ago when I learned from my first dog, Queenie, that dogs were family. Since that time, I have had a great many teachers, both canine and human, who collectively have brought me to this point in my life. To all of them I say, "Thank you." I especially thank Mary Falcon, my editor at Barron's, for deftly and patiently guiding me through the publishing process. Finally, I offer my loving thanks to my children, Christian and Aylecia, who persuaded me—as only children can—to stay home and write, and to my husband, Jim, whose steadfast faith in my capabilities is both gratifying and puzzling.

Important Note

This pet owner's guide tells the reader how to buy and care for a miniature schnauzer. The author and the publisher consider it important to point out that the advice given in the book is meant primarily for normally developed puppies from a good breeder—that is, dogs of excellent physical health and good character.

Anyone who adopts a fully grown dog should be aware that the animal has already formed its basic impressions of human beings. The new owner should watch the animal carefully, including its behavior toward humans, and should meet the previous owner. If the dog comes from a shelter, it may be possible to get some information on the dog's background and peculiarities there. There are dogs that, as a result of bad experiences with humans, behave in an unnatural manner or may even bite. Only people that have experience with dogs should take in such animals.

Caution is further advised in the association of children with dogs, in meeting with other dogs, and in exercising the dog without a leash.

Even well-behaved and carefully supervised dogs sometimes do damage to someone else's property or cause accidents. It is therefore in the owner's interest to be adequately insured against such eventualities, and we strongly urge all dog owners to purchase a liability policy that covers their dog.

Cover Photos

Cheryl A. Ertelt: inside front cover, inside back cover; Isabelle Francais: front cover; Shutterstock: back cover.

Photo Credits

Kent Akselsen: pages 14, 18, 46, 52, 54, 69, 74, 76 (bottom), 77; Cheryl A. Ertelt: pages 2–3, 15, 16, 26, 40, 41, 73, 79, 90, 93; Kent Dannen: pages 5, 11, 12, 13, 21, 24, 27, 33, 34, 35, 36, 42, 62, 67, 80, 85, 89; Tara Darling: pages 4, 8, 10, 17, 72, 78, 84, 86, 92; Isabelle Francais: pages 7, 20, 23, 29, 49, 51, 53, 59, 75; Pet Profiles: pages 31, 81, 83; Pets by Paulette: pages 6, 19, 30, 44, 76 (top), 87; Shutterstock: page 38; Connie Summers/Paulette Johnson: page 71.

All inquiries should be addressed to:
Barron's Educational Series, Inc.
250 Wireless Boulevard
Hauppauge, NY 11788
www.barronseduc.com

ISBN-13: 978-0-7641-4245-1
ISBN-10: 0-7641-4245-3

Library of Congress Control No. 2009927379

Printed in China
9 8 7 6 5 4 3 2 1